HBR Guide to **Better Business Writing**

it's not what you said, but HOW u said it
before send: is this me, at my best?
don't over-explain; reader will stop....
no more than 3 points any topic
outline in complete sentences only (→ complete thoughts, not scraps; so can help be clear...)
edit: tighten, sharpen + brighten

Harvard Business Review Guides

Arm yourself with the advice you need to succeed on the job, from the most trusted brand in business. Packed with how-to essentials from leading experts, the HBR Guides provide smart answers to your most pressing work challenges.

The titles include:

HBR Guide to Better Business Writing

HBR Guide to Finance Basics for Managers

HBR Guide to Getting the Mentoring You Need

HBR Guide to Getting the Right Job

HBR Guide to Getting the Right Work Done

HBR Guide to Giving Effective Feedback

HBR Guide to Making Every Meeting Matter

HBR Guide to Managing Stress at Work

HBR Guide to Managing Up and Across

HBR Guide to Persuasive Presentations

HBR Guide to Project Management

Other Books Written or Edited by Bryan A. Garner

Garner's Modern American Usage

Garner's Dictionary of Legal Usage

Black's Law Dictionary (all editions since 1996)

Reading Law: The Interpretation of Legal Texts, with Justice Antonin Scalia

Making Your Case: The Art of Persuading Judges, with Justice Antonin Scalia

Garner on Language and Writing

The Redbook: A Manual on Legal Style

The Elements of Legal Style

The Chicago Manual of Style, Ch. 5, "Grammar and Usage" (15th & 16th eds.)

The Winning Brief

Legal Writing in Plain English

Ethical Communications for Lawyers

Securities Disclosure in Plain English

Guidelines for Drafting and Editing Court Rules

The Oxford Dictionary of American Usage and Style

A Handbook of Basic Legal Terms

A Handbook of Business Law Terms

A Handbook of Criminal Law Terms

A Handbook of Family Law Terms

HBR Guide to **Better Business Writing**

Bryan A. Garner

HARVARD BUSINESS REVIEW PRESS

Boston, Massachusetts

Printed in the United States of America

10 9 8 7

Library of Congress Cataloging-in-Publication Data

Garner, Bryan A.
HBR guide to better business writing / Bryan A. Garner.
p. cm. — (Harvard business review guides)
Includes bibliographical references and index.
ISBN 978-1-4221-8403-5 (alk. paper)
1. Commercial correspondence. 2. Business writing. I. Harvard business review. II. Title. III. Title: Guide to better business writing.
HF5718.3.G37 2013
808.06′665—dc23

2012032809

The paper used in this publication meets the requirements of the American National Standard for Permanence of Paper for Publications and Documents in Libraries and Archives Z39.48-1992.

MIX
Paper from responsible sources
FSC® C101537
FSC
www.fsc.org

To J.P. Allen,
my lifelong friend

What You'll Learn

Do you freeze up when writing memos to senior executives? Do your reports meander and raise more questions than they answer for key stakeholders? Do your e-mails to colleagues disappear into a void, never to be answered or acted on? Do your proposals fail to win clients?

You'll lose a lot of time, money, and influence if you struggle with business writing. And it's a common problem. Many of us fumble for the right words and tone in our documents, even if we're articulate when we speak. But it doesn't have to be that way. Writing clearly and persuasively requires neither magic nor luck. It's a skill—and this guide will give you the confidence and the tools you need to cultivate it.

You'll get better at:

- Pushing past writer's block.
- Motivating readers to act.
- Organizing your ideas.
- Expressing your main points clearly.

- Cutting to the chase.
- Holding readers' attention.
- Writing concise, useful summaries.
- Trimming the fat from your documents.
- Striking the right tone.
- Avoiding grammar gaffes.

Contents

Introduction: Why you need to write well

You may think you shouldn't fuss about your writing—that good enough is good enough. But that mind-set is costly. Supervisors, colleagues, employees, clients, partners, and anyone else you communicate with will form an opinion of you from your writing. If it's artless and sloppy, they may assume your thinking is the same. And if you fail to convince them that they should care about your message, they *won't* care. They may even decide you're not worth doing business with. The stakes are that high.

Some people say it's not a big deal. They may feel complacent. Or they may think it's ideas that matter—not writing. But good writing gets ideas noticed. It gets them realized. So don't be misled: Writing well *is* a big deal.

Those who write poorly create barriers between themselves and their readers; those who write well connect with readers, open their minds, and achieve goals.

All it takes is a few words to make a strong impression, good or bad. Let's look at four brief passages—two effective and two not. See whether you can tell which ones are which:

1. In the business climate as it exists at this point in time, one might be justified in having the expectation that the recruitment and retention of new employees would be facilitated by the economic woes of the current job market. However, a number of entrepreneurial business people have discovered that it is no small accomplishment to add to their staff people who will contribute to their bottom line in a positive, beneficial way.

2. In this job market, you might think that hiring productive new employees would be easy. But many entrepreneurs still struggle to find good people.

3. The idea of compensating a celebrity who routinely uses social media to the tune of thousands of dollars to promote one's company by tweeting about it may strike one as unorthodox, to say the least. But the number of businesses appropriating and expending funds for such activities year on year as a means of promotion is very much on the rise.

4. Paying a celebrity thousands of dollars to promote your company in 140-character tweets

> may seem crazy. But more and more businesses are doing just that.

Can you tell the difference? Of course you can. The first and third examples are verbose and redundant. The syntax is convoluted and occasionally derails. The second and fourth examples are easy to understand, economical, and straightforward. They don't waste the reader's time.

You already recognize business writing that gets the job done—and trust me, you can learn to produce it. Maybe you think writing is a bother. Many people do. But there are time-tested methods for reducing the worry and labor. That's what you'll find in this book, along with lots of "before" and "after" examples that show these methods in action. (They're adapted from real documents, but disguised.)

Good writing isn't an inborn gift. It's a skill you cultivate, like so many others. Anyone of normal athletic ability can learn to shoot a basketball or hit a golf ball reasonably well. Anyone of normal intelligence and coordination can learn to play a musical instrument competently. And if you've read this far, you can learn to write well—probably very well—with the help of a few guiding principles.

Think of yourself as a professional writer

If you're in business, and you're writing anything to get results—e-mails, proposals, reports, you name it—then you're a professional writer. Broadly speaking, you belong to the same club as journalists, ad agencies, and book authors: Your success may well depend on the writing you produce and its effect on readers. That's why what you produce should be as polished as you can make it.

Here's an example you may be familiar with. Various versions of this story exist—it's sometimes placed in different cities and told with different twists:

> *A blind man sits in a park with a scrawled sign hanging from his neck saying, "I AM BLIND," and a tin cup in front of him. A passing ad writer pauses, seeing only three quarters in the cup. He asks, "Sir, may I change your sign?" "But this is my sign. My sister wrote it just as I said." "I understand. But I think I can help. Let me write on the back, and you can try it out." The blind man hesitantly agrees. Within two hours the cup is full of coins and bills. As another passerby donates, the blind man says: "Stop for a moment, please. What does my sign say?" "Just seven words," says the newest contributor: "It is spring, and I am blind."*

It matters how you say something.

Read carefully to pick up good style

To express yourself clearly and persuasively, you'll need to develop several qualities:

- An intense focus on your reason for writing—and on your readers' needs.
- A decided preference for the simplest words possible to express an idea accurately.

- A feel for natural idioms.
- An aversion to jargon and business-speak.
- An appreciation for the right words in the right places.
- An ear for tone.

How can you acquire these traits? Start by noticing their presence or absence in everything you read. Slow down just a little to study the work of pros. This shouldn't be a chore, and it shouldn't be squeezed in at the end of a long day. Grab a few spare minutes, over your morning coffee or between tasks, and read closely. Find good material that you enjoy. It could be the *Economist* or the *Wall Street Journal,* or even *Sports Illustrated,* which contains tremendous writing.

If you can, read at least one piece aloud each day as if you were a news announcer. (Yes, literally aloud.) Read with *feeling.* Heed the punctuation, the phrasing, the pacing of ideas, and the paragraphing. This habit will help cultivate an appreciation of the skills you're trying to acquire. And once you've honed your awareness, all you need is practice.

Recognize the payoff

An ambiguous letter or e-mail message will require a "corrective communication" to clear up a misunderstanding—which saps resources and goodwill. A poorly phrased and poorly reasoned memo may lead to bad decision-making. An ill-organized report can obscure important information and cause readers to overlook vital facts. A heavy, uninviting proposal will get put aside and forgotten. A badly drafted pitch to a key client will only consume the time of higher-ups who must rewrite it at the eleventh hour to make it passable—lowering its chances of success because of the hectic circumstances surrounding its preparation.

That's a lot of wasted time—and a drag on profits. But you can prevent these problems with clear, concise writing. It's not some mysterious art, secret and remote. It's an indispensable business tool. Learn how to use it, and achieve the results you're after.

One prefatory note: Asterisks are used in the text throughout this book to mark examples of incorrect English grammar, spelling, or usage.

Section 1
Delivering the Goods Quickly and Clearly

Chapter 1
Know why you’re writing

Many people begin writing before they know what they’re trying to accomplish. As a result, their readers don’t know where to focus their attention or what they’re supposed to do with the message. So much depends on your *purpose* in writing that you must fix it firmly in your mind. What do you want the outcome to be? Do you want to persuade someone to sign a franchise contract, for instance? Or to stop using your trademark without permission? Or to come to a company reception?

Say clearly and convincingly what the issue is and what you want to accomplish. With every sentence, ask yourself whether you’re advancing the cause. That will help you find the best words to get your message across.

Form follows function

Say your firm rents space in an office building that has thoroughly renovated the entrance and the entire first floor. Your general counsel has alerted you that the landlord has violated the Americans with Disabilities Act (ADA). For example, there are no wheelchair-access ramps or automatic doors. You've decided to write to the landlord. But *why* are you writing? The answer to that question determines much of what you'll say and *all* of the tone that you'll use. Consider three versions of the letter you might write:

Version #1

You're good friends with the landlord, but you think that the law should be followed for the good of your employees and your customers. Purpose: to gather more information. Tone: friendly.

> Dear Ann:
>
> The new foyer looks fantastic. What a great way for us and others in the building to greet customers and other visitors. Thank you for undertaking the renovations.
>
> Could it be that the work isn't finished? No accommodations have yet been made for wheelchair accessibility—as required by law. Perhaps I'm jumping the gun, and that part of the work just hasn't begun? Please let me know.
>
> Let's get together for lunch soon.
>
> All the best,

Version #2

You're on good terms with the landlord, but on principle, you don't like being in a building that isn't ADA-compliant. You have a disabled employee on staff, and you want the situation righted. Purpose: to correct the oversight. Tone: more urgent.

Dear Ann:

Here at Bergson Company, we were delighted when you renovated the first floor and made it so much more inviting to both tenants and visitors. We are troubled, however, by the lack of wheelchair-access ramps and automatic doors for handicapped employees and customers, both of which are required by state and federal law. Perhaps you're still planning that part of the renovations. If so, please advise.

If this was a mere oversight, can you assure us that construction on ramps and automatic doors will begin within 60 days? Otherwise, as we understand it, we may be obliged to report the violation to the Vermont Buildings Commission. Without the fixes, you may be subject to some hefty fines—but we feel certain that you have every intention of complying with the law.

Sincerely,

Version #3

You've had repeated problems with the landlord, and you have found a better rental property elsewhere for your company. Purpose: to terminate your lease. Tone: firm, but without burning bridges.

Dear Ms. Reynolds:

Four weeks ago you finished renovating the first floor of our building. Did you not seek legal counsel? You have violated the Americans with Disabilities Act—as well as state law—by failing to provide a wheelchair-access ramp and automatic doors for handicapped visitors and employees. Because four weeks have elapsed since you completed the work, we are entitled under state law to terminate our lease. This letter will serve as our 30 days' notice.

Although we have no doubt that your oversight was a good-faith error, we hope that you understand why we can't stay in the building and have made plans to go elsewhere.

We hope to remain on friendly terms during and after the move.

Sincerely,

These three letters are quite different because you are writing them to accomplish different things. Focus on the reaction you're trying to elicit from the reader. You want results. Yet notice how even the sternest letter—Version 3—maintains a civil tone to foster goodwill. No hostility is necessary.

Recap

- Consider your purpose and your audience *before* you begin writing, and let these guide both what you say and how you say it.
- Plainly state the issue you're addressing and what you hope to achieve.
- Keep your goal in mind: Don't undermine your efforts with a hostile or inappropriate tone.

Chapter 2
Understand your readers

Communication is a two-way exercise. Without knowing something about your readers—and about psychology in general, for that matter—you'll rarely get your ideas across. What are their goals and priorities? What pressures do they face? What motivates them?

Respect readers' time constraints

The most important things to realize about all business audiences are these:

- Your readers are busy—*very* busy.
- They have little if any sense of duty to read what you put before them.
- If you don't get to your point pretty quickly, they'll ignore you—just as you tend to ignore long, rambling messages when you receive them.

- At the slightest need to struggle to understand you, they'll stop trying—and think less of you.
- If they don't buy your message, you may as well have stayed in bed that day.

Each of these universal tendencies becomes magnified as you ascend the ranks of an organization. Your job as a writer, then, is to:

- Prove quickly that you have something valuable to say—valuable to *your readers,* not just to you.
- Waste no time in saying it.
- Write with such clarity and efficiency that reading your material is easy—even enjoyable.
- Use a tone that makes you likable, so that your readers will want to spend time with you and your message.

Do these things and you'll develop a larger reservoir of goodwill. You'll not only have a genuinely competitive edge, but you'll also save time and money.

Tailor your message

If you're writing a memo to colleagues, for example, consider where they sit in the organization and what they're expected to contribute to its success. Or if you're responding to a client's request for proposal, address every need outlined in the RFP—but also think about the client's industry, company size, and culture. Your tone will change depending on your recipients, and so will your content. You'll highlight the things they care about most—the ever-important "what's in it for them."

Connect with particular readers to connect with large audiences

It's challenging to write for a large, diverse group of readers, especially if you don't know them. But you can make it easier by focusing on some specific person you know. In his preface to the U.S. Securities and Exchange Commission's *Plain English Handbook,* Warren Buffett suggests grounding your prose by having a particular reader in mind:

> When writing Berkshire Hathaway's annual report, I pretend that I'm talking to my sisters. I have no trouble picturing them: Though highly intelligent, they are not experts in accounting or finance. They will understand plain English, but jargon may puzzle them. My goal is simply to give them the information I would wish them to supply me if our positions were reversed. To succeed, I don't need to be Shakespeare; I must, though, have a sincere desire to inform.

If you focus on a smart nonspecialist who's actually in your audience—or, like Buffett, imagine that you're writing for a relative or a friend—you'll strike a balance between sophistication and accessibility. Your writing will be more appealing and more persuasive.

Your readers may have little or no prior knowledge about the facts or analysis you're disclosing. But assume that they're intelligent people. They'll be able to follow you if you give them the information they need, and they won't be bamboozled by empty, airy talk.

NOT THIS:	BUT THIS:
We aspire to be a partner primarily concerned with providing our clients the maximal acquisition of future profits and assets and focus mainly on clients with complex and multi-product needs, large and midsized corporate entities, individual or multiple entrepreneurial agents, and profit-maximizing institutional clients. By listening attentively to their needs and offering them paramount solutions, we empower those who wish to gain access to our services with the optimal set of decisions in their possible action portfolio given the economic climate at the time of the advice as well as the fiscal constraints that you are subject to. Against the backdrop of significant changes within our industry, we strive to ensure that we consistently help our clients realize their goals and thrive, and we continue to strengthen the coverage of our key clients by process-dedicated teams of senior executives who can deliver and utilize our integrated business model. On the back of a strong capital position and high levels of client satisfaction and brand recognition, we have achieved significant gains in market share. We hope that you have a favorable impression of our company's quantitative and qualitative attributes and will be inclined to utilize our services as you embark on your financial endeavors.	We're a client-focused firm dedicated to making sure you get the most out of our services. Our client base includes individual entrepreneurs, midsized companies, and large corporations. If you decide to do business with us, we'll give you financial advice that is in tune with the current economy and with what you can afford to invest. For years, we've consistently received the highest possible industry ratings, and we have won the coveted Claiborne Award for exceptional client satisfaction 17 of our 37 years in business. We hope to have the opportunity to work with you in your financial endeavors.

Recap

- Understand that your readers have no time to waste: Get to the point quickly and clearly to ensure that your message gets read.
- Use a tone appropriate for your audience.
- Emphasize the items most important to your readers. If they can easily see how your message is relevant to them, they will be more likely to read it and respond.
- Choose an intelligent, nonspecialist member of your audience to write for—or invent one—and focus on writing for that person. Your message will be more accessible and persuasive to all your readers as a result.

Chapter 3

Divide the writing process into four separate tasks

Do you feel anxious every time you sit down to write? Your main difficulty is probably figuring out how to begin. Don't try to picture the completed piece before you've gathered and organized your material. It's much too soon to think about the final, polished product—and you will just make the challenge ahead of you seem overwhelming. The worry can take more out of you than the actual writing.

Instead, break up your work. Think of writing not as one huge task but as a series of smaller tasks. The poet, writer, and teacher Betty Sue Flowers has envisioned them as belonging to different characters in your brain: MACJ.[1] That stands for Madman–Architect–Carpenter–

1. Betty S. Flowers, "Madman, Architect, Carpenter, Judge: Roles and the Writing Process," *Proceedings of the Conference of College Teachers of English* 44 (1979): 7–10.

Judge, representing the phases that a writer must go through:

- **The Madman** gathers material and generates ideas.
- **The Architect** organizes information by drawing up an outline, however simple.
- **The Carpenter** puts your thoughts into words, laying out sentences and paragraphs by following the Architect's plan.
- **The Judge** is your quality-control character, polishing the expression throughout—everything from tightening language to correcting grammar and punctuation.

You'll be most efficient if you carry out these tasks pretty much in this order. Sure, you'll do some looping back. For example, you may need to draft more material after you've identified holes to fill. But do your best to compartmentalize the discrete tasks and address them in order.

Get the Madman started

Accept your good ideas gratefully whenever they come. But if you're methodical about brainstorming at the beginning of the process, you'll find that more and more of your good ideas will come to you early—and you'll largely prevent the problem of finally thinking of your best point after you've finished and distributed your document.

Get your material from memory, from research, from observation, from conversations with colleagues and others, and from reasoning, speculation, and imagination. The problem you're trying to solve may seem intractable, and you may struggle to find a good approach. (How on earth will you persuade the folks in finance to approve your budget request when they're turning down requests left and right? How will you get the executive board to adopt a new mind-set about a proposed merger?) Don't get hung up on the size of the challenge. Gathering ideas and facts up front will help you push through and defuse anxiety about the writing.

How do you keep track of all this preliminary material? In the old days, people used index cards. (I wrote my first several books that way.) But today the easiest way is to create a rough spreadsheet that contains the following:

- Labels indicating the points you're trying to support.
- The data, facts, and opinions you're recording under each point—taking care to put direct quotes within quotation marks.
- Your sources. Include the title and page number if citing a book or an article, the URL if citing an online source. (When writing a formal document, such as a report, see *The Chicago Manual of Style* for information on proper sourcing.)

As you're taking notes, distinguish facts from opinions. Be sure to give credit where it's due. You'll run aground if you claim others' assertions as your own, because you'll probably be unable to back them up convincingly. Worse, you'll be guilty of plagiarism.

This groundwork will save you loads of time when you're drafting and will help you create a well-supported, persuasive document.

Let the Architect take the lead

You may feel frustrated at first as you're groping for a way to organize your document. If a sensible approach doesn't come to mind after you've done your research and scouted for ideas, you may need to do more hunting and gathering. You want to arrive at the point of writing down three sentences—complete propositions—that convey your ideas. Then arrange them in the most logical order from the reader's point of view (see chapter 4). That's your bare-bones outline, which is all you typically need before you start drafting.

Give the Carpenter a tight schedule

The key to writing a sound first draft is to write as swiftly as you can (you'll read more about this in chapter 5). Later, you'll make corrections. But for now, don't slow yourself down to perfect your wording. If you do, you'll invite writer's block. Lock the Judge away at this stage, and try to write in a headlong rush.

Call in the Judge

Once you've got it all down, it's time for deliberation—weighing your words, filling in gaps, amplifying here and curtailing there. Make several sweeps, checking for one thing at a time: the accuracy of your citations, the tone, the quality of your transitions, and so on. (For an editorial checklist, see chapter 6.) If you try to do many things at once, you won't be doing any of them superbly. So leave plenty of time for multiple rounds of editing—at least as much time as you spent researching and writing. You'll ferret out more problems, and you'll find better fixes for them.

Recap

- Approach a writing project as a series of manageable tasks using the MACJ method.
- Use the Madman to gather research and other material for the project, diligently keeping track of quotations and sources. And allow more of your best ideas to come early by methodically brainstorming at the beginning of the process.
- As the Architect, organize the Madman's raw material into a sensible outline. Distill your ideas into three main propositions.
- In the Carpenter phase, write as quickly as possible—without worrying about perfecting your prose.
- Finally, assume the role of the Judge to edit, polish, and improve the piece. Do this in several distinct passes, each time focusing on only one element of your writing.

1st: rough, loose ideas (Slt — in Madman phase

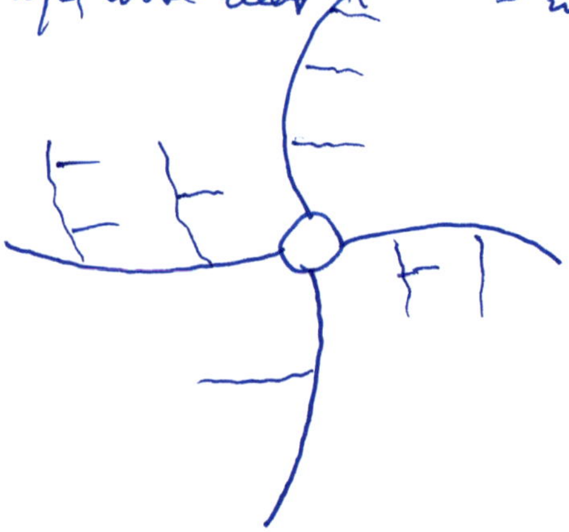

2nd: digest into 3 main propositions, full sentences (good incl. "because") in Architect phase
[Title]

Chapter 4
Before writing in earnest, jot down your three main points—in complete sentences

A mathematician once told me that there are really only four numbers in the world: one, two, three, and many. There's something to that: Four items just seem to be one too many for most people to hold in their memory. But a proposal, a report, or any other piece of business writing feels underdeveloped when it's supported by only one or two points.

So write down your three main points as full sentences, and spell out your logic as clearly as you can. That way, you'll force yourself to think through your reasons for recommending a vendor, for example, or pitching an offer to a client—and you'll make a stronger case.

If you try to simply think things out as you write, you'll run into trouble because you won't really know yet what you're hoping your reader will think or do. You'll flail about, gradually clarifying your point as you make several runs at it. In the end, after multiple attempts, you may finally figure out what you have to say, but you probably won't say it in a way that your reader can follow.

An example of finding your focus

Let's say your name is Carol Sommers, and you work at a small management-consulting firm. Your boss, Steve, owns the business and is considering acquiring a 17,000-square-foot building as his new office. Because you're the office manager, Steve has asked you to think through the logistics and to write up your recommendations before the company makes an offer to purchase the building. At first, you're at a loss—there are so many issues to sort through. But you've got to start somewhere.

So before you write your memo, you put on your Madman hat and brainstorm a list of considerations:

- Ownership
- Maintenance
- Buildout
- Security
- Offices vs. cubicles
- Real-estate values—comparables?

- The move—bids on movers?
- Timing
- Tax consequences
- Employee and visitor parking
- Environmental inspection and related issues
- Smooth transitioning: phone and Internet service, mail forwarding, new stationery, updating business contacts, subscriptions, etc.
- Insurance
- Leaving current landlord on good terms
- Taking signage to new location?

These are just *topics,* not fully formed thoughts. But now that you have a rough list, you can start the Architect phase of writing and categorize in threes.

Steve's responsibilities (before acquisition):

- Consider an environmental inspection to make sure that the building has no hidden issues. Our commercial realtor can help.
- Check with our accountant to find out what tax consequences we might have depending on how we time the closing.
- Ask the accountant and perhaps a tax lawyer whether Steve should own the property personally, whether the company should own it, or whether a

newly formed entity (an LLC, for example) should own it. There may be liability issues.

My responsibilities (before acquisition):

- Cost out insurance coverage.
- Interview contractors for building out the space to our satisfaction. (Note to self: Confirm that we can roll the buildout into the mortgage.)
- Cost out the annual bill for providing the kind of security we currently have.

My responsibilities (postacquisition):

- Contract for maintenance (cleaning and trash services, lawn and parking-lot care).
- Plan the move, with a smooth transition in operations (the physical move, mail forwarding, phone and Internet, new stationery, address updates, announcement to customers, moving signage, etc.).
- Help Steve plan the architectural buildout to foster collaboration and use space efficiently.

To come up with all this, put yourself in Steve's place, imagining what you'd want *your* office manager to think of to help you do your job better. But it also takes a little legwork—for example, talking to people at firms that have recently changed locations or acquired buildings. Can't find anyone like that through your network? Ask the commercial realtor to put you in touch with one or two of its clients.

For each stage, we've listed the three big issues—at least what we *think* they are. Look how easy it is now to begin your Carpenter work (writing a useful memo to Steve):

Memo

To: Steve Haskell
From: Carol Sommers

Re: The Prospective Purchase of 1242 Maple Avenue
Date: April 12, 2012

As you requested, I've thought through the logistics of purchasing and moving into the Maple Avenue property. Here are my suggestions for each stage of the process.

Now

I'd like your approval to tackle the following tasks immediately because they'll give us a more complete picture of how expensive the acquisition and move would be:

- Cost out insurance coverage.
- Interview contractors for building out the space to our satisfaction. (I've checked with the bank to see if we can roll the buildout into the mortgage, and we can.)
- Cost out the annual bill for providing the kind of security we currently have.

Preclosing

If you decide to go forward with the purchase and your offer is accepted, I'll take care of these items before we close on the loan:

- Arrange for at least one thorough inspection of the building.
- Work with our accountant, to the extent you'd like, to get papers in order for obtaining the bank financing you mentioned.
- Ensure that all due-diligence deadlines are met.

After Closing

After closing, I'll get into the nuts and bolts of the move:

- Help you plan the architectural buildout to foster collaboration and use space efficiently.
- Plan the move, with a smooth transition in operations (the physical move, mail forwarding, phone and Internet, new stationery, address updates, announcement to customers, moving signage, etc.).
- Contract for maintenance (cleaning and trash services, lawn and parking-lot care).

Issues for You to Think About

While I'm attending to the details above, you might want to:

- Consider environmental and structural inspections to make sure the building has no hidden issues. Our commercial realtor says he can provide guidance—I'd be happy to set up a meeting if you like.
- Check with our accountant to find out what tax consequences we might have depending on how we time the closing.
- Ask the accountant and perhaps a tax lawyer whether you should own the property person-

> ally (highly unlikely), whether Haskell Company should own it, or whether a newly formed entity (such as an LLC) should own it. You or the company may face liability issues with outright ownership.

Of course, I'm always on hand to take on whatever tasks you need. Just let me know.

Prewriting in threes resulted in a clear, useful memo. It helped us forestall writer's block, organize the material, and make concise, well-reasoned recommendations.

But did you notice that the finished memo breaks things down into four categories, not three? As hard as I tried to think of everything before writing the memo, I couldn't. Looking at my preliminary list, I identified a gap in time—a period in which there would be other necessary tasks. So I added the preclosing category and wrote those items on the fly. But I probably wouldn't have come up with them if I hadn't started with a plan. Organizing my main points in sets of three helped me see the preclosing gap; after that, filling it in wasn't difficult.

The order of categories changed, too. Why move Steve's tasks from the beginning to the end? The memo was about what you, Carol Sommers, the office manager, could do for Steve. To think of your responsibilities, you needed to think of Steve's. That was your starting point for brainstorming—but not for your memo.

You couldn't very well lead by telling your boss what he needs to do. That's not your place, and that's not what he asked for. So Steve's to-dos can go at the end, as helpful reminders. That way, you can focus his attention mainly on items you'll take care of to make his decisions easier.

Recap

- Find your focus by first generating a list of topics to cover.
- Develop these raw ideas into full sentences and categorize your main points in sets of three.
- Arrange these sets in a logical order, keeping your reader's needs in mind.

Chapter 5
Write in full—rapidly

Once you've written your three main points so that you know where you're going, you're in Carpenter mode—ready to put together the ideas you've generated and organized. Write as quickly as possible. Your sentences will be shorter than they otherwise would be, your idioms will be more natural, and your draft should start taking shape before you know it. If there's a painful part of writing, it's doing the first draft. When you shorten the duration, it's not as painful.

Time yourself

To prevent premature fussing, write against the clock. (Creative writers call this speed writing. They often use it as an exercise to get juices flowing.) Allow yourself 5 or 10 minutes to draft each section—the opener, the body, and the closer—and set the timer on your computer or phone to keep yourself honest.

Don't edit as you go

It's counterproductive to allow the Judge and the Carpenter to work side by side. That's essentially multitasking—you're just doing two things inefficiently rather than simultaneously. And besides, the editorial part of the brain is simply incompatible with the production part. Who needs a fault-finding critic's kibitzing when you're trying to create something new and fresh? You're best off keeping the Judge away as you produce your first draft. You'll spend plenty of time editing later.

Don't wait for inspiration

Inspiration rarely comes when you want it to. After the careful planning you've done, you won't need it anyway. As the management expert Peter Drucker famously said about innovation, good writing takes careful, conscious work, not a "flash of genius."

If you follow the MACJ process, you'll inspire *yourself*—and minimize your procrastinating. Once the Madman and the Architect have worked, you should be primed to write. Schedule the time when the Carpenter is to begin, and when the appointed time comes, get started.

Begin by writing in support of what you're most comfortable addressing. When you get stuck, skip to something else. You need to get into a flow. If you're still struggling when you come back to that problem passage, say out loud (to yourself or to a colleague) what you're trying to convey. Sometimes speaking will help you find the right words. The point is to get your ideas on paper—knowing that you'll still have time to elaborate and perfect them at the next stage.

Recap

- Write your first draft as quickly as you can.
- Don't get stuck waiting for inspiration. Try giving yourself 5 to 10 minutes for each section when drafting.
- Resist the urge to perfect as you write. Saving the editing until the draft is finished will keep the Judge from getting in your way.
- Schedule a time for the Carpenter to work—and when that time comes, begin.
- If you find yourself stumped, move on to a different section you're more comfortable with and come back to the problem once you've found your flow.

Chapter 6
Improve what you've written

Once you've written a complete draft, you'll revise first and then edit. Revising is a reconsideration of what you're saying as a whole, and where you're saying it. It's rethinking the floor plan. Editing is more a matter of fine-tuning sentences and paragraphs. You need to allow time for both. On the one hand, don't let some neurotic obsession with perfectionism delay important projects. On the other hand, don't rashly send things out without proper vetting and improvement.

Revising

As a reviser, you're asking several questions:

- Have I been utterly truthful?
- Have I said all that I need to say?
- Have I been appropriately diplomatic and fair?

- Do I have three parts to the piece—an opener, a middle, and a closer?
- In my opener, have I made my points quickly and clearly? And concretely?
- Have I avoided a slow wind-up that unnecessarily postpones the message?
- In the middle, have I proved my points with specifics?
- Is the structure immediately apparent to my readers? Have I used informative headings?
- Is my closer consistent with the rest—yet expressed freshly? Have I avoided lame repetition?

Editing

When it comes to editing, you're asking different questions as you read through your sentences and paragraphs:

- Can I save some words here?
- Is there a better way of phrasing this idea?
- Is my meaning unmistakable?
- Can I make it more interesting?
- Is the expression relaxed but refined?
- Does one sentence glide into the next, without discontinuities?

An example of revising and editing

To understand the process more concretely, let's take a look at how an internal memo takes shape through three drafts. The first draft is not very clear and omits important information, but the germ of an idea is there:

First Draft

To: All Sales Personnel
From: Chris Hedron
Subject: Changes in Order-Processing Procedure

In order to facilitate the customers' placement of orders, a new order-processing procedure has been designed. The process will require a customer to enter the product and/or service code into our order-entry system, which will then generate a quote for the job and return it to the customer for approval. This will make time for the customer to review the quote and transmit any changes before work begins. Upon receipt of the customer's written approval, the quote will be transformed into a work order. This procedure will make it easier and faster for us to process customers' orders.

This memo needs some amplification, especially in the realms of who, what, why, and when. The second draft, a full-fledged revision, fleshes out much that was unclear about the first draft.

Second Draft

To: All Sales Personnel
From: Chris Hedron
Subject: New Work-Order-Processing Procedure

Because our current work-order-processing procedure requires a lot of paperwork and phone calls, it's difficult for customers to make changes prior to the commencement of work. The procedure is inefficient and subject to numerous errors. And it takes up to four weeks from quote to approval to work order. So we have designed a new four-step order-processing procedure that will allow customers to place orders through our website and allow us to begin jobs faster.

Beginning in January 2013, we will inform our customers about the new procedure, and on April 20, 2013, we will implement the new procedure, which will work as follows. First, to initiate or change a work order, customers can visit our website to request a quote by filling out a detailed form and providing a purchase-order number. Second, we will transmit a quote to the customer for approval. Third, if the customer approves, they can return the quote with an electronic signature and purchase-order number. Fourth, we will transform the quote to a work order immediately. Work-order changes can be made using the same procedure except that instead of a quote, customers will request a work-order change.

The focus there was on saying all that needed to be said—not on refining the expression. Now, though, it's possible to engage in fine-tuning and to produce a much-improved draft.

Third Draft

To: All Sales Personnel
From: Chris Hedron
Subject: New Work-Order-Processing Procedure

Our current work-order processing takes a lot of paperwork and phone calls, so it's hard for our customers to make changes to the work before it begins. The procedure is inefficient and subject to error. And it takes up to four weeks from quote to approval to work order. We have therefore designed a new four-step procedure that has two key benefits: (1) Customers can place orders through our website, and (2) we can start jobs faster.

Beginning January 2013, we'll tell our customers about the new procedure. On April 20, 2013, we'll implement it. The new procedure will work in four steps:

- Customers can visit our website to request a quote for a job by filling out a form and providing a purchase-order number.
- We'll then send a quote for the customer's approval.
- The customer can return the approved quote with a digital signature.
- We'll instantly convert the quote to a work order.

Work-order changes can be made using the same procedure except that instead of a quote, customers will request a work-order change.

Recap

- Allow yourself ample time to revise and edit your work.

- Consider your draft in its entirety. Take a fresh look at your content and structure: Have you said everything you need to—and in the most effective way?

- Then edit your work, fine-tuning to tighten, sharpen, and refine your prose.

Chapter 7

Use graphics to illustrate and clarify

When you're writing about complex ideas, for example, or looking for useful ways to break up a long stretch of text, you can use a simple, elegant chart to convey critical information at a glance. Such graphics especially serve people who want to skim what you've written.

A few crucial principles:

- Make sure your graphics illustrate something discussed in the text.
- Place them near the text they illustrate, preferably on the same page or on a facing page.
- Use legends and keys that readers can easily grasp.

To learn how to produce effective graphics, consult the books of Edward Tufte, especially *Envisioning*

Information and *Beautiful Evidence*. You'll marvel at the amount of learning and the sophisticated thought that lie behind superb visuals.

It would be gross negligence to leave off without a graphic, so here's one to round out the section. Note that when you flip through this book, your eye stops here. That's because any departure from the norm achieves a special emphasis. If every third or fourth page had such a

FIGURE 7-1

The Who-Why-What-When-How Chart

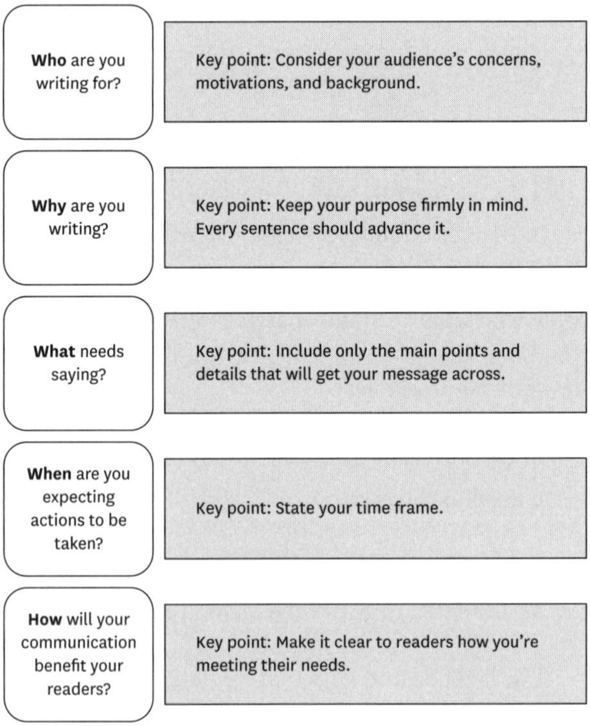

chart, the effect would be nullified. So make your graphics distinctive—and don't overuse them.

Recap

- Distill your report (or part of it) into a chart, diagram, or other visual aid that helps your audience understand the content and its import.
- Take your design cues from visuals you have found effective.
- Read the books of Edward Tufte to develop this skill.

Section 2
Developing Your Skills

3 goals as edit:
tighten – fewer
sharpen – clearer words, show, more precise, specific
brighten – more interesting words, less monotonous

pretend to be someone else, w/ different point(s) of view

serial edits from several – scheduled
don't add time to discuss – just decide

Chapter 8
Be relentlessly clear

Clarity can be a double-edged sword. When you're forthright enough to take a position or recommend a course of action, you're sticking your neck out. People who don't want to commit make their writing muddy. Perhaps they're trying to leave room for their views to evolve as events unfold. Or perhaps they're hoping they can later claim credit for good results and deny responsibility for bad ones.

The fact is, though, that many readers will perceive them not as savvy wait-and-see participants but as spineless herd-followers who are slow to see (much less seize) opportunities within their reach. So clean up the mud.

Adopt the reader's perspective

Always judge clarity from the reader's standpoint—not your own. Try showing a draft to colleagues with fresh eyes and asking them what they think your main points are. If they can't do that accurately, then you're not being clear enough.

Your ideal should be to write so unmistakably that your readers can't possibly misunderstand or misinterpret. Anything that requires undue effort from them won't be read with full attention—and is bound to be misunderstood.

Keep your language simple

Simplicity breeds clarity. Strive to use short words and sentences. Over the years, research has confirmed again and again that the optimal average for readable sentences is no more than 20 words. You'll need variety to hold interest—some very short sentences and some longer ones—but aim for an average of 20 words. With every sentence, ask yourself whether you can say it more briefly.

NOT THIS:	**BUT THIS:**
Efficiency measures that have been implemented by the company with strong involvement of senior management have generated cost savings while at the very same time assisting in the building of a culture that is centered around the value of efficiency. We anticipate that, given this excising of unnecessary expenditures and enhanced control of other expenditures, the overall profitability of the company will be increased in the near term of up to four quarters.	Our senior management team has cut costs and made the company more efficient. We expect to be more profitable for the next four quarters.

If you're writing about technical matters for an audience of nonspecialists—for example, explaining the benefits of a software upgrade to end users or putting together an investment primer for your company's 401(k) participants—don't try to define each term in the sentence where it first appears. That will bulk up your sentences and make the material even harder for people to grasp. Sometimes you'll need a new sentence or even a new paragraph to explain a term or concept in simple, straightforward English.

Show, don't tell

You probably heard writing teachers in school say, "Show, don't tell." It's excellent advice no matter what you're writing—even business documents. The point is to be specific enough that you lead your readers to draw their own conclusions (conclusions that match yours, of course), as opposed to simply expressing your opinions without support and hoping people will buy them.

Consider these examples:

NOT THIS:	**BUT THIS:**
He was a bad boss.	He got a promotion based on his assistant's detailed reports, but then—despite the company's record profits—denied that assistant even routine cost-of-living raises.
The company lost its focus and floundered.	The CEO acquired five unrelated subsidiaries—as far afield as a paper company and a retailer of children's toys—and then couldn't service the $26 million in debt.
The shares of OJM stock issued to Pantheon stockholders in the merger will constitute a significant proportion of the outstanding stock of OJM after the merger. Based on this significant proportion, it is expected that OJM will issue millions of OJM shares to Pantheon stockholders in the merger.	We expect that OJM will issue about 320 million shares of its stock to Pantheon shareholders in the merger. That figure will account for about 42% of OJM's outstanding stock after the merger.

WRITE LETTERS TO SHARPEN YOUR SKILLS

Your letter writing is the best barometer of your writing skills generally. And it's a safe way to practice—to prepare yourself for your more difficult writing tasks. Write thank-you letters, congratulatory letters, letters of recommendation (when asked), complaint letters, letters to the editor, personal notes (handwritten), and all sorts of others. If you can write good letters, you can write just about anything. (See chapter 19, "Business Letters," for pointers on how.) That's because they help you to focus on *others*. When you write a letter, you're connecting with one particular recipient. And letters help you build goodwill with people. An e-mail message may create an impression, but it's far less likely to be remembered than a personal letter is.

To develop the habit, try writing a few letters a week. Make many of them handwritten notes. (When you receive one in a stack of mail, isn't that the first thing that grabs your attention?) They're personal and, if well done, memorable and even savable. They'll help you build and maintain relationships. Write them to tell those you supervise how much you appreciate their hard work, congratulate colleagues on promotions, motivate team members to meet goals, let new partners know you're eager to start collaborating, and so on. To write a good one, keep it neat, try limiting it to one page, make it warm and friendly, use *you* more than *I*, and use tasteful, mature stationery.

A short, vague sentence (like "He was a bad boss") may register in the readers' minds—but only as a personal impression that's potentially biased. It's credible only if its source is highly credible. As for the long, vague sentence about OJM stock, there's nothing for readers to hold on to, and they'll get tired trying.

Concrete business writing is persuasive because it's evidence-based, clear, and memorable. When you supply meaningful, objective details (explaining, for example, that the floundering company "couldn't service the $26 million in debt"), you're sharing information, not just your opinion that the company "lost its focus." You earn credibility by demonstrating a command of the facts. You also give your message staying power. People don't care about—or even remember—abstractions the way they do specifics.

So if you're marketing your firm's consulting services to potential clients, don't just tell them you'll save them money. Say how much money you've saved others. Don't just promise that you'll make their lives easier. List the time-consuming tasks you'll take off their hands. Don't just claim to have deep experience in the health care industry. *Name names:* Mention several hospitals and medical centers you've done work for, and include testimonials saying how happy clients are with the time and money you've saved them.

Recap

- Put yourself in the reader's shoes to assess your clarity. Better yet, see whether a colleague can accurately summarize the main points of your draft from a quick read-through.

- Phrase your ideas as plainly and briefly as possible, aiming for an average sentence length of 20 or fewer words.
- Pave your readers' way with concrete details. Don't try to push them there with abstract assertions.
- Cultivate your letter writing to improve your writing skills more generally.

Chapter 9

Learn to summarize—accurately

A good summary is focused and specific—and it's at the beginning of your document so readers don't have to dig. It gets to the point. It lays the foundation for what's to follow. There's no holding back on the crucial information.

Consider the difference between these two openers to a recommendation that a proposal be rejected:

NOT THIS:

Summary

The cell phone changeover that has been proposed should be rejected. For the reasons stated below, the company would not be well served by accepting the proposal.

BUT THIS:

Summary

Last year, we adopted an officewide policy of issuing cell phones to all executives and sales reps at an annual cost of $58,000 (including voice and data plans). The Persephone company has proposed that we switch to its phones and service at an annual cost of $37,000. The committee charged with evaluating this proposal recommends that we reject it for four reasons:

1. The new plans would have significantly less coverage in Europe and Asia, so our international sales reps might suffer lost opportunities.
2. Our current provider has been highly responsive and has tailored its service to our needs.
3. The $21,000 savings is dwarfed by potential costs (even one dropped sales call could result in a loss of much more money than that).
4. Persephone's customer service appears from credible online reviews to be inferior.

What makes the second version better? It can be fully understood by anyone who reads it—at any time. The first version, by contrast, assumes familiarity: It's clear to only a few "insiders"—and for only a limited period. And because it's vague, it lacks the credibility that the second version earns through specifics.

Struggling to incorporate the right amount of detail to make your summary clear and useful? Write a descriptive outline of your document—summarize each paragraph or section with a sentence that captures the who, what, when, where, why, and how—and try creating your overall summary out of that. Also, keep your readers' needs foremost in your mind. What questions will people have when they open your document? Provide brief but concrete answers to those questions. These will assure readers that what follows will matter to them.

Be brief—but not too brief

People often assume that shorter is better when it comes to summaries. But brevity without substance is worthless. Never say more than the occasion demands—but never say less, either. Adopt the reader's perspective: Fill in as much information as it takes to get people up to speed. Think of your summary as the CliffsNotes version of your document. Although the second example is longer, it conveys the whole gist of the message. And there's not one wasted word, which brings us to our next chapter.

Recap

- Summarize the vital information at the beginning of the document.
- Summarize each section with a sentence that addresses "the five Ws" (who, what, when, where, why) and how—and use these sentences to build your general summary.
- Provide only the information the reader needs to understand the issue—no more and no less.

= tightening

Chapter 10
Waste no words

Make every word count. When you mean *before,* don't say or write *prior to,* much less *prior to the time when.*

Though *prior to* is a linguistic choice that the dictionary offers us, it's a bad choice. Never use two words for one, three words for two, and so on. Syllables add up fast and slow people down. Of course, stick to idiomatic English. Don't start dropping articles (*a, an, the*) where we'd all normally expect them. And don't cut the important word *that* left and right—more often than not, you really need it to be clear. But remove all the words that aren't performing a real function. Doing so saves readers time and effort and makes your ideas easier to grasp and apply.

Wordiness can exist on many levels, from rambling statements to unnecessary repetition to verbose expressions that could be replaced by shorter, sharper alternatives. Whatever the manifestation, it's bad. Consider the following examples:

NOT THIS:	BUT THIS:
The trend in the industry is toward self-generation by some companies of their own websites, and Internet technology is changing the nature of training necessary to acquire the skill of website development at an acceptable level of sophistication, so that this activity can more and more be handled in-house. [49 words]	Since Internet technology makes it easier than ever to develop sophisticated websites, some companies now develop their own in-house. [19 words]
We are unable to fill your order at this point in time because there is an ongoing dock strike that affects our operations. [23 words]	We cannot fill your order right now because of the dock strike. [12 words]
I am writing in response to a number of issues that have arisen with regard to the recent announcement that there will be an increase in the charge for the use of our lobby computers. [35 words]	You may have heard that we're raising the fees for using our lobby computers. [14 words]
The greater number of these problems can readily be dealt with in such a way as to bring about satisfactory solutions. [21 words]	Most of these problems can be readily solved. [8 words]

To trim extra words from your documents, try:

- Deleting every preposition that you can, especially *of:* change *April of 2013* to *April 2013* and *point of view* to *viewpoint.*

- Replacing every *–ion* word with a verb if you can. Change *was in violation of* to *violated* and *provided protection to* to *protected.*

- Replacing *is, are, was,* and *were* with stronger verbs where you can. Change *was hanging* to *hung* and *is indicative of* to *indicates.*

You'll see all three tricks at work here:

NOT THIS:	**BUT THIS:**
The manufacturers of tools for gardening have been the victims of a compression factor that has resulted in an increase in units on the market accompanied by a negative disproportionate rise of prices. [36 words]	The garden-tool industry has suffered from an oversupply of units coupled with rising prices. [14 words]
For the near and intermediate future in terms of growth goals, Bromodrotics, Inc., is evaluating its corporate design needs. The purpose of this short-term and intermediate-term evaluation is to make a determination as to how the image of the company might best be positioned to be of assistance to the sales force in meeting its growth goals. [57 words]	To increase sales, Bromodrotics needs to improve its image. [9 words]

Ruthlessly cut words from your first draft, so long as you remain faithful to the sounds and rhythms of normal, down-to-earth English. Don't compress words to the point of sounding curt or unnatural.

One other trick in that last example: eliminating padding such as *in terms of* and *the purpose of.* Sometimes you'll find even worse phrases:

in this connection it might be observed that

it is important to bear in mind that

it is interesting that

it is notable that

it is worthwhile to note that

it should be pointed out that

it will be remembered that

Leave all these things unsaid—without saying *it goes without saying that . . . .*

Recap

- Never use more words than necessary: If you can say it in two words instead of three, do so—as long as the result still sounds natural.
- Tighten your prose by removing inessential prepositions, replacing abstract *-ion* nouns with action verbs where possible, and replacing wordy *be*-verb phrases with more direct simple verbs.
- Eliminate padding that doesn't contribute to your meaning.

Chapter 11

Be plain-spoken: Avoid bizspeak

It's mission-critical to be plain-spoken, whether you're trying to be best-of-breed at outside-the-box thinking or simply incentivizing colleagues to achieve a paradigm shift in core-performance value-adds. Leading-edge leveraging of your plain-English skill set will ensure that your actionable items synergize future-proof assets with your global-knowledge repository.

Just kidding. Seriously, though, it's important to write plainly. You want to sound like a person, not an institution. But it's hard to do, especially if you work with people who are addicted to buzzwords. It takes a lot of practice.

Back when journalists were somewhat more fastidious with the language than they are today, newspaper editors often kept an "index expurgatorius": a roster of words and phrases that under no circumstances (except perhaps in a damning quote) would find their way into print. Here's such a list for the business writer. Of course, it's just a starting point—add to it as you come across other examples of bizspeak that hinder communication by substituting clichés for actual thought.

Bizspeak Blacklist

actionable (apart from legal action)

agreeance

as per

at the end of the day

back of the envelope

bandwidth (outside electronics)

bring our A game

client-centered

come-to-Jesus

core competency

CYA

drill down

ducks in a row

forward initiative

going forward

go rogue

guesstimate

harvesting efficiencies

hit the ground running

impact (as verb)

incent

incentivize

impactful

kick the can down the road

Let's do lunch.

Let's take this offline.

level the playing field

leverage (as verb)

liaise

mission-critical

monetize

net-net

on the same page

operationalize

optimize

out of pocket (except in reference to expenses)

paradigm shift

parameters

per

planful

pursuant to

push the envelope

putting lipstick on a pig

recontextualize

repurpose

rightsized

sacred cow

scalable

seamless integration

seismic shift (outside earthquake references)

smartsized

strategic alliance

strategic dynamism

synergize; synergy

think outside the box

throw it against the wall and see if it sticks

throw under the bus

turnkey

under the radar

utilization; utilize

value-added

verbage (the correct term is *verbiage*—in reference only to verbose phrasings)

where the rubber meets the road

win-win

These phrases have become voguish in business—abstain if you can. Sometimes people use them to enhance their own sense of belonging or to sound "in the know." Or they've been taught that good writing is hyperformal, so they stiffen up when they use a keyboard or pick up a pen, and they pile on the clichés.

It takes experience to bring your written voice into line with your spoken voice and to polish it so well that no one notices the polish.

NOT THIS:	**BUT THIS:**
The reduction in monthly assessments which will occur beginning next month has been made financially feasible *as a result of leveraging* our substantial reductions in expenditures.	We'll be cutting your assessments beginning next month because we've saved on expenses.
It is to be noted that a considerable amount of savings has been made possible *by reason of our planful initiation of* more efficient and effective purchasing procedures.	We've saved considerable sums by streamlining our purchases.

Hunt for offending phrases

Start looking for bizspeak in all kinds of documents, from memos to marketing plans, and you'll find it everywhere. You'll eventually learn to spot it—and avoid it—in your own writing. You'll omit canned language such as *Attached please find* and other phrases that only clutter your message.

Bizspeak may seem like a convenient shorthand, but it suggests to readers that you're on autopilot, thoughtlessly using boilerplate phrases that people have heard over and over. Brief, readable documents, by contrast, show care and thought. *Attached please find* is just one example among many:

NOT THIS:	**BUT THIS:**
at your earliest convenience	as soon as you can
in light of the fact that	because
we are in receipt of	we've received
as per our telephone conversation on today's date	as we discussed this morning
Pursuant to your instructions, I met with Roger Smith today regarding the above-mentioned.	As you asked, I met with Roger Smith today.
Please be advised that the deadline for the above-mentioned competition is Monday, April 2, 2012.	The deadline is April 2, 2012.
Thank you for your courtesy and cooperation regarding this matter.	Thank you.
Thank you in advance for your courtesy and cooperation in this regard. Please do not hesitate to contact me if you have any questions regarding this request.	Thank you. If you have any questions, please call.

Writing plainly means expressing ideas as straightforwardly as you can—without sacrificing meaning or tone.

Take Warren Buffett again, one of the smartest business leaders on the planet—and someone, by the way, who cares a lot about good business writing. Consider how he rewrote a short passage that he found in a financial-services firm's business prospectus. Read through the first excerpt before you read Buffett's translation below it, and note the bizspeak phrases that landed on the cutting-room floor as Buffett tightened and translated:

NOT THIS:

Maturity and duration management decisions are made *in the context of* an intermediate maturity orientation. The maturity structure of the portfolio is adjusted *in the anticipation of* cyclical interest-rate changes. Such adjustments are not made *in an effort to* capture short-term, day-to-day movements in the market, but instead *are implemented in anticipation of* longer-term, secular shifts in the interest rates (*i.e.*, shifts transcending *and/or* not inherent to the business cycle). Adjustments made to shorten portfolio maturity and duration are made to limit capital losses during periods when interest rates are expected to rise. Conversely, adjustments made to lengthen maturation for the portfolio's maturity and duration strategy lies *in the analysis of* the U.S. and global economies, focusing on levels of real interest rates, monetary and fiscal policy actions, and cyclical indicators.

Words: 136
Sentences: 5 (All passive voice)
Average sentence length: 27.2
Flesch Reading Ease: 8.2

BUT THIS:

We will try to profit by correctly predicting future interest rates. When we have no strong opinion, we will generally hold intermediate-term bonds. But when we expect a major and sustained increase in rates, we will concentrate on short-term issues. And conversely, if we expect a major shift to lower rates, we will buy long bonds. We will focus on the big picture and won't make moves based on short-term considerations.

Words: 74
Sentences: 5 (None passive voice)
Average sentence length: 14.8
Flesch Reading Ease: 60.1

If you analyze the before-and-after prospectuses under the Flesch Reading Ease (FRE) scale—a test developed by readability expert Rudolf Flesch to measure the comprehensibility of written passages using word and sentence length—you can quantify the difference. The higher the score, the easier the passage is to read and comprehend. On a scale of 0–100, the original 136-word prospectus on top scores an 8.2. In contrast, Warren Buffett's revision below it scores a 60.1. To give some perspective, *Reader's Digest* scores 65 on the FRE scale, *Time* magazine around 52, and the *Harvard Law Review* in the low 30s. Increasing a passage's readability is not the same as "dumbing it down." The revised passage above gives the reader the same information—but more clearly.

Here's a shorter example, this time from a community college's mission statement:

NOT THIS:

The object of this enterprise is *to facilitate the development of greater capacities* for community colleges and not-for-profit neighborhood organizations to *engage in heightened collaboration in regard to the provision of* community services that would *maximize the available resources* from a number of community stakeholders and to *provide a greater level of* communication about local prioritization of educational needs with the particular community.

[63 words]

BUT THIS:

This project seeks to help community colleges and nonprofit neighborhood groups work more efficiently together.

[15 words]

In both the Buffett example and the community-college example, the original versions seem to be aiming at something other than getting the point across. Perhaps the writers wanted to sound impressive, or wanted to obscure what they were actually up to, or wanted to cover up the fact that they weren't entirely sure what they were up to. Whatever the answer, the original styles won't work on any target audience.

Recap

- Aim to write as naturally as you speak: Sound like a human being, not a corporation.
- Avoid boilerplate phrases that weigh down your language and suggest lazy thinking.
- Increase readability by expressing your ideas as directly as possible.

Chapter 12

Use chronology when giving a factual account

Stories are inherently chronological. One thing happens, then another, then another. That structure works well not only in books and films but also in business writing. It's more likely to be clear and efficient, and to keep readers interested. So include "just the facts, ma'am," as Joe Friday on the old TV series *Dragnet* used to say. Just the facts that *matter*, and in the right order.

In theory this point seems obvious, but in practice writers find storytelling difficult. They often dive straight into the middle without orienting their readers, and the inevitable result is confusion on the receiving end. You're familiar with this phenomenon. It happens all the time in conversations with friends or family members: "Wait a minute. Back up. When was this? Where were you? And why were you talking to this guy? And where'd he come from?"

Suppose you're sending an e-mail message to give the status of an ongoing project, and it's been some time since the last update. The recipient isn't as immersed in the project as you are and probably has many other things going on. So remind your reader where things stood when you last communicated about the subject, and describe what's happened since then:

NOT THIS:	**BUT THIS:**
Sarah— It was hard making headway with Jim Martinez, but finally we're looking (in the best-case scenario) at a demonstration of what our software can do by mid-May, as I established in my first telephone conference with Jim last Monday at 9:00 a.m. He was out Wednesday and Thursday (I didn't see any reason to try calling on Tuesday), but on Friday he told me that we'd need a sample app. But prior to that, Magnabilify requires an NDA. Tuesday's meeting should clarify things. Let me know what you think. Frank	Sarah— Last week you asked me to approach Magnabilify Corporation, the software developers, to see whether they might have any interest in our customizing some security applications for their computer systems. I finally got through to Jim Martinez, corporate vice president in charge of software, and we have planned a face-to-face meeting at his office next Tuesday. The next steps, as I understand them under Magnabilify's protocol, will be to enter into a nondisclosure agreement, to develop a sample application (in less than two weeks), and to schedule a demonstration shortly after. Can you and I chat before Tuesday's meeting? Frank

The version on the left reads like stream-of-consciousness. The writer didn't take the time to step back, think of the message from the reader's perspective, and then lay out the important points chronologically. A story, even a short one like the narrative on the right, holds the reader's interest more effectively than jumbled facts interspersed with opinions.

Plot out what happened, and when

When a serious dispute arises within a company, the lawyers will typically ask their clients to produce a "chronology of relevant events," detailing the most important incidents leading up to the dispute. This document helps everyone involved think more clearly about how things unfolded. Try taking a similar approach when writing a document that walks the reader through a series of events—whether you're sending someone a project update or preparing an employee's performance evaluation. Create a chronology of relevant events to organize the narrative. Say you did that before drafting your e-mail message to Sarah in the right-hand example. Here's how it might look:

Chronology of relevant events

Last week	Sarah asked me to gauge Magnabilify's interest in having us build customized security applications.
Today	I spoke with Jim Martinez.
Next Tuesday	Jim and I will meet at his office to discuss.
In two weeks	If Magnabilify is interested, we'll do an NDA, develop a sample app, and schedule a demo.

Once you've laid out the chronology like this, drafting the e-mail message becomes a lot easier—just a matter of stringing the events together and asking to meet with Sarah before next Tuesday's meeting.

Recap

- Include only the relevant facts.
- Provide them in chronological order to make it easy for your readers to follow you.
- Organize your narrative by creating a chronology of relevant events before you write; then string the events together in your draft. But avoid the rote recitation of unnecessary dates.

Chapter 13

Be a stickler for continuity

Smooth writing consists of a sequence of well-joined sentences and paragraphs, not a mere collection of them. This smooth sequencing requires good planning and skill in handling transitions, or links that help readers follow your train of thought.

Watch how a good writer on business ethics, Manuel G. Velasquez, does it with a series of paragraph openers (the links are indicated here by italics):

A Series of Paragraph Openers from Manuel G. Velasquez's* Business Ethics *(2011)

1. *How well* does a free monopoly market succeed in achieving the moral values that characterize perfectly competitive free markets? Not well.

2. The *most obvious failure* of monopoly markets lies in the high prices they enable the

monopolist to charge and the high profits they enable him to reap, a failure that violates capitalist justice.

3. A monopoly market *also* results in a decline in the efficiency with which it allocates and distributes goods.

4. *First,* the monopoly market allows resources to be used in ways that will produce shortages of those things buyers want and cause them to be sold at higher prices than necessary.

5. *Second,* monopoly markets do not encourage suppliers to use resources in ways that will minimize the resources consumed to produce a certain amount of a commodity.

6. *Third,* a monopoly market allows the seller to introduce price differentials that block consumers from putting together the most satisfying bundle of commodities they can purchase given the commodities available and the money they can spend.

7. Monopoly markets *also* embody restrictions on the negative rights that perfectly free markets respect.

8. A monopoly market, *then,* is one that deviates from the ideals of capitalist justice, economic utility, and negative rights.

The italicized transitional phrases steer us from one idea to the next. Normally, we wouldn't even notice them. The transitions in really good writing are almost subliminal—but they're carefully placed where readers will need them. These connections take readers forward in different ways. They can:

- **Establish a time sequence:** *then, at that point, afterward, as soon as, at last, before, after, first, initially, meanwhile, later, next, now, once, originally, since, then, until, finally*

- **Establish place:** *there, in that place, at the front, in back, farther back, in the rear, at the center, to the left (right), up front, way back*

- **Add a point:** *and, or, further, also, in fact, moreover, not only . . . but also*

- **Underscore a point:** *above all, after all, and so, chiefly, equally important, more so, indeed, more important*

- **Concede a point:** *although, and yet, admittedly, at the same time, certainly, even though, doubtless, granted, no doubt, of course, still, though, to be sure, whereas, yet, while*

- **Return to a point:** *even so, nevertheless, nonetheless, still*

- **Give an example:** *for example, for instance, in particular*

- **Provide a reason:** *because, hence, thus, for, it follows, since, so, then, therefore*

- **Set up a contrast:** *but, yet, and yet, conversely, despite, by contrast, instead, on the other hand, still, then, while*

- **Set up a conclusion:** *so, as a result, finally, in conclusion, in short, in sum, on the whole, therefore, thus, to sum up*

Use subheads as transitions

No matter how smooth your transitions are between sentences and paragraphs, time-pressed readers will zone out if you place a solid wall of text in front of them. Break up your documents (even e-mails that are longer than a paragraph) with some signposts to lead people from section to section and help them quickly locate the parts they're particularly interested in. A "summary" subhead, for example, tells readers where to find just the highlights. And subheads that concisely yet clearly lay out your key points allow people to skim and still get the gist of your message.

Make your subheads as consistent as you can. For instance, if you're leading a task force that's recommending ways to forge direct customer relationships through social media, you might write each subhead in your body text as a directive, along these lines:

Use LinkedIn to Get Feedback on Current Products

Use Facebook to Test New Concepts

Use Twitter to Facilitate Chats About Live Events

The parallelism will help your document hang together both rhetorically and logically.

Recap

- Use well-placed transitional phrases to guide the reader to your next idea and indicate its relationship to what came before.
- Break up documents with concise, descriptive subheads to increase readability and help readers quickly locate the information most important to them.
- Use a "summary" subhead to point your readers to the document's highlights.
- Use consistent style and parallel syntax in your subheads to reinforce the document's logical and rhetorical cohesion.

Chapter 14
Learn the basics of correct grammar

Why nitpick about grammar? Because readers may see your language—especially your use of your native language—as a reflection of your competence. Make lots of mistakes and you'll come across as uneducated and uninformed. People will hesitate to trust your recommendation to launch a resource-intensive project, for example, or to buy goods or services. They may think you don't know what you're talking about.

Telltale indicators

Consider pronouns. If you don't know how to handle *I* and *me,* many of your colleagues, partners, and customers won't take you seriously. Some errors will predictably get you in trouble:

- "She placed an order *with Megan and I." (Correct: She placed an order with Megan and me.)
- (On the phone:) "*This is him." (Correct: This is he.)

- "Just keep this matter *between you and I." (Correct: Just keep this matter between you and me.)
- "*Whom may I say is calling?" (Correct: Who may I say is calling?)

The rule, very simply, is that *I, we, he,* and *she* are subjects of clauses <Leslie and I were delighted to work with you>; *me, us, him,* and *her* are objects of either verbs or prepositions <Please call either Leslie or me> <You might want to consult with Leslie and me>. In the compound phrasings, try leaving out *Leslie and*—and you'll know the correct form immediately.

Besides pronoun problems, here are the main types of grammatical errors to watch out for. As for dozens of other wording issues that can torpedo your credibility, see Appendixes D and F.

Subject-verb disagreement

A verb must agree in person and number with its subject <I am aware of that> <You are aware of that> <Pat is aware of that> <We are all aware of that>. But syntax can make things tricky.

There is poses a problem because *There* appears to be the subject. It's not. It's what grammarians call an expletive—not a bad-word expletive (as in "expletive deleted"), but a word that stands in for the subject in an inverted sentence. In these sentences, *there is* just means "exists." Take, for example, *There is a vacancy on the hiring committee.* The uninverted sentence would be *A vacancy (exists) on the hiring committee.* Because *there* seems to some people to resemble a singular subject, they tend to use a singular verb. But *there* inverts the word order, and the true subject follows the verb <There are several reasons for approving the plan>. And, of course, when the subject is plural, a plural verb is needed.

NOT THIS:	BUT THIS:
There *is* always risk and liability *considerations* to take into account.	There *are* always risk and liability *considerations* to take into account.
There *is* many *options* to avoid a takeover.	There *are* many *options* to avoid a takeover.

Another troublesome area for subject–verb disagreement involves prepositional phrases that follow the subject. By "false attraction," they often mislead writers to choose the wrong verb (singular for plural or vice versa). The object of a prepositional phrase is never the subject of a sentence. It may be nearer the verb, but the number of the subject controls the number of the verb:

NOT THIS:	BUT THIS:
The *details* of the customized work *is delaying* the project.	The *details* of the customized work *are delaying* the project.
The *source* of our replacement parts and maintenance *have not been selected* yet.	The *source* for our replacement parts and maintenance supplies *has not been selected* yet.

In the first example, *work* is the object of the preposition *of,* so the plural subject *details* controls the verb. In the second, *source* takes the singular *has not been selected.*

Disagreements can also arise with compound subjects connected by *or, either . . . or,* or *neither . . . nor.* If the subjects are all singular then the verb is singular as well. But when one or more are plural, the number of the verb must match the number of the noun that follows the *or* or *nor*:

NOT THIS:	BUT THIS:
Special services *or* a new product *target* a niche market.	Special services *or* a new product *targets* a niche market.
Neither the education fund *nor* the training costs *is* without budget constraints.	Neither the education fund *nor* the training costs *are* without budget constraints.

In the first example, the singular subject *a new product* after the *or* mandates a singular verb. In the second example, the plural subject after *nor* makes the verb plural as well. Notice that it's more idiomatic to use the *singular subject or plural subject + plural verb* form.

Noun-pronoun disagreement

Strictly speaking, a pronoun must have the same gender and number as the subject.

NOT THIS:	BUT THIS:
A shareholder may cast *their* vote for only one member of the board.	*A shareholder* may cast *his or her* vote for only one member of the board.

Although *their* is colloquially used as a genderless singular pronoun, this usage is not yet widely accepted in formal writing. And unless you know the sex of the subject, try to avoid using a masculine or feminine pronoun. If you wish to make a political statement with pronoun gender (by always choosing the generic feminine, for example), do so: Just know that some of your readers may be distracted by it or may discount your credibility. The safest course is to use some ingenuity to write in an invisibly gender-neutral way.

NOT THIS:	BUT THIS:
Either the receptionist or the sales assistant will have to change *their* lunch hour so that at least one will be in the office at all times.	*Either* the receptionist or the sales assistant will have to start taking lunch earlier or later so that at least one will be in the office at all times.
Three candidates responded to the advertisement for the financial-officer position. *Each* submitted *their* résumé.	*Three candidates* responded to the advertisement for the financial-officer position. *Each* submitted *a* résumé.

But back to grammar. When the subject of a sentence is a singular pronoun such as *either, neither, each,* or *every,* other nouns that accompany it have no effect on the number of the verb:

NOT THIS:	BUT THIS:
Have either of our clients arrived yet?	*Has either* of our clients arrived yet?
Neither of the new products have sold spectacularly this year.	*Neither* of the new products *has* sold spectacularly this year.
Each of us *are* responsible for the tasks assigned.	*Each* of us *is* responsible for the tasks assigned.

Double negatives

A double negative occurs when back-to-back negatives are meant to intensify, not cancel, each other. It's easy to recognize in dialect (for example, *we didn't have no choice* or *it didn't hardly matter*), but the problems can be more subtle in formal writing. Watch for the word *not* plus another word with a negative sense.

NOT THIS:	BUT THIS:
We *couldn't scarcely* manage to keep up with the demand.	We *could scarcely* manage to keep up with the demand.

Another subtle double-negative combination is *not . . . but.*

NOT THIS:	BUT THIS:
The clerk *couldn't* help *but* call the manager for advice.	The clerk *couldn't* help calling the manager for advice.

But indicates a negative or contradiction, so *not . . . but* may be ambiguous. The first sentence could mean the clerk had some other option. The second sentence clearly states there was no alternative.

Nonstandard vocabulary

In business writing, always use standard English—unless you're writing specifically for a niche audience of nonstandard speakers. Broadly speaking, standard English is characterized by attention to accepted conventions for grammar, vocabulary, spelling, and punctuation.

You needn't always be strictly formal—in appropriate situations, use less formal English. But your prose and speech must always be professional and respectful.

Dialect is always nonstandard. Avoid using it in business:

NOT THIS:	BUT THIS:
Where's the meeting *at?*	*Where's* the meeting?
Me and Kim will handle the Brewster account.	*Kim and I* will handle the Brewster account.

Nonstandard language may also creep in when writers rely on the spoken sounds of words:

NOT THIS:	**BUT THIS:**
They *shouldn't of* submitted those incomplete reports.	They *shouldn't have* submitted those incomplete reports.

Irregular verbs are also fertile ground for nonstandard language.

NOT THIS:	**BUT THIS:**
We *drug* our heels getting into the mid-Atlantic market.	We *dragged* our heels getting into the mid-Atlantic market.
Our late entry almost *sunk* our chances against established competitors.	Our late entry almost *sank* our chances against established competitors.

How to correct yourself

Here are three good ways to brush up: (1) Read first-rate nonfiction; (2) have knowledgeable colleagues proof your material and explain their corrections; and (3) browse through guides on grammar and usage, consulting them whenever questions arise.

This last method will help you distinguish between the real rules and the artificial ones that plague so much writing. For example, were you told in school never to begin a sentence with a conjunction? So was I. But look at all the *and*s and *but*s that begin sentences in first-rate prose. They're everywhere. These words, as sentence-starters, keep readers going smoothly with the train of thought. They don't break any real rules—and they never have.

Grammatically, there's nothing wrong with using *additionally* and *however* as sentence-starters. But stylistically, they're inferior. The multisyllable connectors don't join as cleanly and as tightly as monosyllables do.

Do you worry that your readers will *think* a sentence-starting conjunction is wrong? They won't even notice it, just as you never do. Good style gets readers focused on your clear, concise message. Bad style, by contrast, draws attention to itself.

For a handy collection of grammar guidelines, see Appendix B, "A Dozen Grammatical Rules You Absolutely Need to Know." And be sure to spend some quality time with Appendix F, "A Primer of Good Usage." Fall in love with the language, and it will love you back.

Recap

- When considering verb number, watch for compound subjects, inverted syntax, and prepositional phrases that follow the subject.

- Never mistake the object of a preposition for the subject of a sentence.

- Avoid using *they/them/their* as genderless singular pronouns in formal writing.

- Avoid double negatives.

- Follow the conventions of standard English.

- Improve your grasp of standard English by reading quality nonfiction, having colleagues review your writing, and referring to grammar and usage guides when you have questions.

Chapter 15
Get feedback on your drafts from colleagues

Say you've drafted a budget request. Ask people on your team to read it and make sure you've explained clearly, concisely, and persuasively why you should receive the funding, for example, to hire two more staff members. And if possible, get constructive feedback from an objective peer in a different department—preferably someone who is good at lobbying for resources.

Pay attention to what your colleagues say: Their reactions will probably be quite close to those of your intended readers.

Accept suggestions graciously

A good writer welcomes good edits—yearns for them, in fact. A bad writer resents them, seeing them only as personal attacks. A good writer has many ideas and tends to value them cheaply. A bad writer has few ideas and values them too dearly. So share your material while it's still rough—the feedback will help you make it shipshape much faster than if you were toiling in isolation.

Try to avoid having your colleagues explain their edits in person. You may get defensive and have a hard time recognizing good advice. Invite them to mark up your document, and thank them for their help.

If you have the people you supervise tightening and brightening your prose regularly, you'll benefit in two ways: Your documents will be more polished, and the people you manage will, with practice, become better editors and writers. Give them direction, though: Ask them to look not just for outright errors but also for passages that are verbose, unclear, or awkwardly expressed. Ideally, you'll get to the point where you're accepting 80 percent of their suggestions.

Create a culture where editing flourishes

At my company, everyone who edits or proofreads must suggest at least two changes per page. No one is allowed to hand something back—even a short letter—and say, "It looks good to me!" People can always make improvements by asking, "What did the writer not say that should have been said? How could the tone be improved? Isn't there a better, shorter way of phrasing one of the ideas?" And so on.

If each reader suggests at least two edits per page, your typos will get caught—believe me. Typos are generally the easiest things to catch, so readers will usually mark those before trying the more difficult task of suggesting stylistic improvements. In the end, awkwardness will disappear. You and your team will look better because you'll *perform* better. You'll make stronger, clearer arguments. You'll put together more persuasive pitches.

Does this seem like overkill? Consider that every communication you send is a commentary on your team or company and its level of professionalism. If it's a printed brochure or a commercial e-mail with wide distribution, the more feedback the better. You simply cannot have too many sets of knowledgeable eyes review the copy.

A dumb mistake can be disastrous—as a major university discovered after printing thousands of commencement brochures with "School of Pubic Affairs" in large type on the front cover. A photo of this embarrassing gaffe almost instantly popped up on the Internet, of course, and the university became the target of many jokes.

When it comes to writing, you want a culture of unneurotic helpfulness. There's no shame in needing edits from others. People should freely seek them and freely give them—without any unpleasant overtones of one-upmanship. Everyone in an organization, regardless of rank, can benefit from good editing.

Recap

- Routinely ask your colleagues and those you supervise to read your drafts and suggest edits.
- Have them mark up the document and submit their edits in writing, rather than explaining them in person, to avoid reacting defensively. Always thank them for their help.
- Foster an environment where edits are freely sought and offered—without overtones of petty one-upmanship.

Section 3
Avoiding the Quirks That Turn Readers Off

Chapter 16

Don't anesthetize your readers

It seems obvious that you shouldn't put your audience to sleep, doesn't it? It should also be obvious to people who talk in circles at dinner parties or deliver dull lectures, but consider how many boring speakers you've had to listen to. It doesn't have to be that way—whether in conversation or in writing.

Ponder the best conversationalists and the best lecturers you've ever heard. No matter how obscure the topic, they make it fascinating through their technique. They avoid trite expressions. They use strong, simple words. Think of Winston Churchill's famous phrase "blood, toil, tears, and sweat." And remember what George Washington reputedly said when questioned about the fallen cherry tree: not "It was accomplished by utilizing a small sharp-edged implement," but "I used my little hatchet."

Effective writers use the same techniques. Why do you read some books all the way through but set others aside?

It's their style: the way they explain things, the way they tell the story.

Here are several tips for writing business documents that hold readers' attention.

Use personal pronouns skillfully

Don't overuse *I* (try not to begin paragraphs or successive sentences with it), but do lean heavily on *we, our, you,* and *your.* Those are personal, friendly words that add human interest and pull readers into a document. Rudolf Flesch, a leading figure in plain-English circles and the author of *How to Be Brief,* was one of the first to explain the need for *you:*

> Keep a running conversation with your reader. Use the second-person pronoun whenever you can. Translate everything into *you* language. *This applies to citizens over 65 = if you're over 65, this applies to you. It must be remembered that = you must remember. Many people don't realize = perhaps you don't realize.* Always write directly to *you,* the person you're trying to reach with your message.

Likewise, the words *we* and *our*—in reference to your firm or company—make corporations and other legal entities sound as if they have collective personalities (as they should and typically do). People usually appreciate this down-to-earth approach over the sterile, distancing effect of third-person prose. Compare the following examples:

NOT THIS:	BUT THIS:
Whether or not *a stockholder* plans to attend a meeting, *he or she* should take the time to vote by completing and mailing the enclosed proxy card to *the Company*. If a *stockholder* signs, dates, and mails a proxy card without indicating how *he or she* wants to vote, *that stockholder's* proxy will be counted as a vote in favor of the merger. If *a stockholder* fails to return a proxy card, the effect in most cases will be a vote against the merger.	Whether or not *you* plan to attend a meeting, please take the time to vote by completing and mailing the enclosed proxy card to *us*. If *you* sign, date, and mail *your* proxy card without indicating how *you* want to vote, *your* proxy will count as a vote in favor of the merger. If *you* don't return *your* card, in most cases *you'll* be counted as voting against the merger.

Use contractions

Many writers have a morbid fear of contractions, having been taught in school to avoid them. But you won't be breaking any real rules if you use them—and they counteract stuffiness, a major cause of poor writing.

This doesn't mean that you should become breezy or use much slang—just that it's good to be relaxed. If you would say something as a contraction, then write it that way. If you wouldn't, then don't.

NOT THIS:	BUT THIS:
For those customers who do not participate in West Bank's online banking program, and do not wish to consider doing so, West Bank will continue sending them statements by U.S. Mail.	If you prefer not to use our online banking program, we'll continue mailing your statements to you.
We would like to remind you that it is not necessary to be present to win. We will inform all winners by telephone subsequent to the drawing.	Remember: You needn't be present to win the drawing. We'll call you if you win.

Stick to simple language

I know I repeat this again and again—but it bears repeating. Readers who can't follow you will stop trying.

Avoid passive voice

Don't say "The closing documents were prepared by Sue," but instead "Sue prepared the closing documents"; not "The message was sent by George," but either "George sent the message" or "The message came from George." This guideline is hardly absolute—sometimes passive voice is the most natural way to say what you're saying. Sometimes it can't be avoided. (See?) But if you develop a strong habit of using active voice, you'll largely prevent convoluted, backward-sounding sentences in your writing.

How do you identify passive voice? Remember that it's invariably a *be*-verb (typically *is, are, was, were*) or *get,* plus a past-tense verb. There are eight *be*-verbs and countless past participles.

Examples of Passive Voice

is + delivered

are + finished

was + awarded

were + praised

been + adjusted

being + flown

be + served

am + relieved

got + promoted

You will improve your writing if you minimize passive voice. (Not: Your writing will be improved if passive voice is minimized by you.)

Vary the length and structure of your sentences

Monotony, as Cicero once said, is in all things the mother of boredom. It's true of syntax no less than it's true of eating or anything else. Sameness cloys. So you want short sentences and long; main clauses and subordinate ones. You want variety.

NOT THIS:	BUT THIS:
Over a significant period of time, we have gained experience helping our clients improve operational performance and maximize both the efficiency of their human resources and the economical utilization of their capital. Ours is an integrated approach that both diagnoses and streamlines operating practices and procedures using lean maintenance and optimization tools, while at the same time implementing change-management techniques involving mind-sets and behaviors of those involved in managerial positions within a given organization.	For many years, we have helped clients better use their resources and improve performance. How? By streamlining operations and changing managers' mind-sets and behaviors.

NOT THIS:	BUT THIS:
In order to provide you, the user of our products, the option of obtaining free replacements for defective products from the nearest office, we offer a simplified processing without acknowledgment of the statutory duty ("goodwill") regardless of whether the product has been purchased there or has reached the user by another route.	What should you do if you need a free replacement for a defective product? Go to the nearest office. Any of our offices can help even if you did not purchase the item there.

Avoid alphabet soup

Readers find acronyms tiresome, especially ones they're not familiar with. So use them judiciously. It might be convenient to refer to COGS instead of spelling out "cost of goods sold." If you also throw in acronyms such as ABC ("activity-based costing"), EBITDA ("earnings before interest, tax, depreciation, and amortization"), and VBM ("value-based management"), the accountants in your audience will follow you—but you'll lose everyone else. Small wonder, too. People don't want to master your arcane vocabulary to get what you're saying.

Surely you've had this experience as a reader: You encounter an acronym (a long one if you're particularly unlucky) and can't connect it with anything you've read in the article or document so far. You find yourself scanning backward through the text, hoping to find the first appearance of that acronym or words that might fit it. By the time you find it (or give up trying), you've completely lost the writer's train of thought. Never put your own readers through that.

Stick to words when you can. Acronyms make writing easier but reading harder. Your shortcut is the reader's hindrance.

Recap

- Don't overuse *I*. Use *we, our, you,* and *your* instead to add a personal touch and appeal to your reader.
- Avoid stuffiness by overcoming any fear you might have of contractions.
- For clearer, more straightforward writing, prefer active voice—unless the passive in a particular context sounds more natural.
- Vary the length and structure of your sentences.
- Make the reader's job easier by avoiding acronyms when you can.

Chapter 17
Watch your tone

Striking the right tone takes work—but it's critical to the success of your business documents. If you sound likable and professional, people will want to work with you and respond to you. So adopt a relaxed tone, as if speaking directly to the recipient of your document.

Avoid hyperformality

What do you think of colleagues who say or write "How may I be of assistance?" instead of "How may I help you?" Or "subsequent to our conversation" instead of "after we spoke"? When they choose overblown words over everyday equivalents, don't they strike you as pompous?

Too much formality will spoil your style. Keep your writing down to earth and achieve a personal touch by:

- Writing your message more or less as you'd say it, but without all the casualisms (*like*s and *you know*s).
- Including courtesies such as *thank you, we're happy to,* and *we appreciate.*

- Using the names of the people you're writing about (*David Green,* not *the above-mentioned patient*).
- Using personal pronouns (*you, he, she*—not *the reader, the decedent, the applicant; we understand*—not *it is understood; we recommend*—not *it is recommended by the undersigned*).

Be collegial

You'll have better luck delivering most kinds of messages, even tough ones, if you approach people collegially. Imagine that everything you write will be paraded before a jury in a contentious lawsuit. You'll want that jury to think you've behaved admirably. Of course, sometimes you'll need to take an aggressive stance—for example, when you're at the last stage before litigation. But do this *only* as a last resort, and preferably on advice of counsel.

Be yourself. Just be your most careful, circumspect self. People have gotten their companies into terrible trouble—and have lost their jobs—by writing ill-considered letters, memos, and e-mails. So always summon your best judgment.

Even if you're collegial and fairly relaxed, your language will vary somewhat depending on your relationship with the recipient. You'll be okay if you ask yourself, "How would I say this to so-and-so if he were right here with me?" You don't want a distant tone with your closest colleagues, and you don't want a chummy tone with someone you don't know all that well.

Never try to make your readers admit that they're in the wrong. It's unwise to say that they *labor under a delusion,* or *claim to understand,* or *fail to understand,* or *complain,* or *erroneously assert,* or *distort.* These expressions, and others like them, breed ill will. Instead, treat your readers with integrity and fairness—and show your willingness to meet them halfway.

Drop the sarcasm

Sarcasm expresses contempt and superiority. It doesn't shame people into compliance. Rather, it's a surefire way of irritating and alienating them. Compare:

NOT THIS:	BUT THIS:
Given that Monday was a bank holiday, as declared by federal statute no less, your e-mail of the 17th of the present month did not come to my attention until yesterday. It is with no small degree of regret that we note that you deemed it necessary to send a follow-up e-mail to us regarding this matter, since we are desirous of establishing a relationship of mutual trust and respect.	Because Monday was a bank holiday, I didn't receive your e-mail message of the 17th until yesterday. Naturally I was chagrined that you had to write a second time. But of course I want you to call on me whenever I might help.

In the left-hand column, note the deadly combination of hyperformality and sarcasm, and the annoying subtext: "You wrote on a holiday, you DOPE. Of course you had to wait for a response." The chance of "establishing a relationship of mutual trust and respect" is very likely diminished.

Recap

- Arrive at a relaxed but professional tone by writing your message as if you were speaking to the recipient in person.
- Refer to people by name, use personal pronouns as you naturally would, and shun fancy substitutes for everyday words.
- Always use your best judgment and a collegial tone in composing your messages, even if the content isn't positive. You'll get better responses from your recipients and keep yourself—and your company—out of trouble.
- Adopt a tone appropriate to your relationship with the recipient.
- Never use sarcasm in professional messages. It will result in a step away from—not toward—your desired outcome.

Section 4

Common Forms of Business Writing

Chapter 18
E-mails

When you send e-mails, do you usually receive a useful, friendly, timely response? Or one that falls short of that ideal? Or no response at all? If you're struggling to get your recipients to focus on your messages, it's because you're competing with a lot of senders—in some cases, hundreds per day.

Here's how to write e-mails that people will actually read, answer, and act on:

- **Get straight to the point—politely, of course—in your first few sentences.** Be direct when making a request. Don't fulsomely butter up the recipient first—although a brief compliment may help ("Great interview. Thanks for sending it. May I ask a favor?"). Spell out deadlines and other details the recipient will need to get the job done right and on time.

- **Copy people judiciously.** Include only those who will immediately grasp why they're on the thread.

And avoid "Reply All." Your correspondent may have been overinclusive with the "Copy" list, and if you repeat that mistake, you'll continue to annoy the recipients who shouldn't be there.

- **Keep your message brief.** People find long e-mails irksome and energy-sapping. The more they have to scroll or swipe, the less receptive they'll be to your message. They'll probably just skim it and miss important details. Many people immediately close long e-mails to read the shorter ones. So rarely compose more than a single screen of reading. Focus your content and tighten your language.

- **Write a short but informative subject line.** With a generic—or blank—subject line, your message will get buried in your recipient's overstuffed inbox. (Not "Program," but "The Nov. 15 Leadership Program.") If you're asking someone to take action, highlight that in the subject line. By making your request easy to find, you'll improve your chances of getting it fulfilled.

- **Stick to standard capitalization and punctuation.** Good writing conventions may seem like a waste of time for e-mail, especially when you're tapping out messages on a handheld device. But it's a matter of getting things right—the little things. Even if people in your group don't capitalize or punctuate in their messages, stand out as someone who does. Rushed e-mails that violate the basic norms of written language bespeak carelessness. And their abbreviated style can be confusing. It takes less time to write a clear message the first time around than it does to follow up to explain what you meant to say.

- **Use a signature that displays your title and contact information.** It should look professional (not too long or ornate) and make it convenient for others to choose how to reach you.

These tips are pretty commonsensical—but they're not common practice. To show you how well they work, let's compare some sample e-mails.

Say you're trying to help a young friend of yours, a budding journalist, land an internship. You happen to know the editor of a metropolitan newspaper, and you send him a message. Consider these two approaches:

NOT THIS:

Subject: Hello there!

Hal—

It's been ages, I know, but I've been meaning to tell you just how effective I think you've been as the editor of the *Daily Metropolitan* these past seven years. Although I canceled my subscription a few years back (LOL)—the papers kept cluttering the driveway—I buy a copy at the coffee shop almost every day, and I always tell people there just how good the paper is. Who knows, I may have won you some subscribers with all my gushing praise! Believe me, I'm *always* touting the good old *DM*.

Anyhoo, I have a mentee I'd like you to meet. You'll soon be thanking me for introducing you to her. She would like an internship, and I know she'll be the best intern you've ever had. Her name is Glenda Jones, and she is A-1 in every way. May I tell her you will contact her? (With good news, I hope!) It can be unpaid. I know your paper has fallen on tough times—but she wants to get into the business anyway! Silly girl. Ah, well, what can you do when journalism seems like it's just in the blood?

Expectantly yours,
Myra

P.S. You'll thank me for this!

BUT THIS:

Subject: Request for an Interview

Hal—

May I ask a favor of you? Glenda Jones, a really sharp mentee in the township's Young Leaders program, wants to pursue a career in journalism, and she's eager to learn how commercial news organizations work. Would you spend 15 minutes chatting with her at your office sometime this month, before school lets out? I know it would be a meaningful introduction for her. You'll find that she is a poised, mature, smart, and incredibly self-possessed young woman.

She tells me that she's looking for an unpaid internship. After a brief interview, perhaps you'd consider giving her a one-week tryout as your assistant. I know you've been a mentor to many aspiring journalists over the years, but here you have a real standout: editor of her college newspaper, Phi Beta Kappa member, state debate champion.

No pressure here. If it's a bad summer for you to take on an intern, I'll completely understand. But please meet with her if you can. I've asked her to write to you independently, enclosing her résumé, to give you a sense of her writing skills.

Thanks very much. Hope you and your family are doing well.

Myra

The first version is colossally ineffective—and if Glenda gets an internship it will be very much *despite* the message from her mentor. The writer is inconsiderate (suggesting that journalism is a thankless career), insensitive (confessing to having canceled her subscription), and horribly presumptuous (acting as if the recipient owes her for "always touting" the newspaper and for suggesting this "A-1" intern—as well as assuming that Glenda must get the job).

The second version is effective because it's humble, *you*-centered, considerate ("No pressure here"), and mildly flattering ("I know you've been a mentor to many"). Though it's a little longer than the first one, it gets to the point sooner, and it provides only helpful information. If

Glenda has any real potential, she stands a decent chance of getting that interview and possibly landing an internship with this version.

You may occasionally need to reprimand someone in an e-mail—to clearly explain a misstep, to make a record of it, or both. Compare these two examples, which show the right and wrong way to deal with an employee who sent an offensive e-mail to the whole team:

NOT THIS:

Subject: You Are in Trouble

Ted—

What on earth were you thinking when you sent that "joke"? Your coworkers sure didn't appreciate it one bit, and neither did I. Don't tell me it was "just a joke." Haven't you cracked your employee handbook and read our company's policies? You've never done this before, that I am aware of. Don't ever send an e-mail like this one again.

Bill Morton
Office Manager

BUT THIS:

Subject: Disruption Caused by Your E-mail

Ted—

What one person considers funny, another may find offensive and insulting. Several people have complained to me about the e-mail headed "Have You Heard This One" that you sent everyone yesterday. I was as upset as they were by the foul language, which is inappropriate for an e-mail sent at work. Our company's policy does not make an exception for offensive language, even when used in jest. Please think about how future e-mails will affect your coworkers. If I receive complaints again, HR will have to get involved. But I trust that won't be necessary.

Bill

In the first version, the writer's anger is clear—and that's about all that's clear. Ted will certainly feel stupid ("What on earth were you thinking" and "Haven't you cracked your employee handbook") and scared ("Don't ever"). But the writer doesn't detail what Ted did wrong and why. And Ted isn't likely to ask ("Don't tell me it was 'just a joke'").

The tone of the second version won't immediately put the recipient on the defensive. This time, the writer explicitly identifies the source of the problem ("the e-mail headed 'Have You Heard This One' that you sent everyone yesterday") and explains the effects, the policy violated, and the consequences. Ted is much more likely to understand his mistake.

Recap

- Be as direct as possible while maintaining a polite tone. Come to the point of your e-mail within the first two or three sentences.

- Never click "Reply All" without first checking the recipient list. Send your e-mail only to people who need to know its contents.

- Keep e-mails brief. Restrict yourself to one screen's worth of text and keep the message tight and focused so your readers get the point fast.

- Write a concise subject line that tells your recipients why you're writing and what it means to them. If they need to act on your message, make that clear in the subject line.

- Diligently adhere to standard writing conventions—even when typing with your thumbs on a handheld device.

Chapter 19
Business Letters

Business letters aren't a quaint thing of the past. They're necessary in all sorts of situations—from correcting a vendor's error to recommending a job candidate to announcing a new service. Effective ones can increase your profitability—by getting key customers to renew large orders, for example, or persuading service providers to charge you less for repeat business. They can also create goodwill, which may eventually yield financial returns.

The pointers in this chapter will help you get those kinds of results.

Use direct, personal language

You see canned phrases like *enclosed please find* and *as per* all the time in letters. They're high-sounding but low-performing. Your letters will be much clearer and more engaging without them.

TIPS FOR WRITING CLEAR, PERSUASIVE LETTERS

- ***Focus on the reader.*** Try not to begin with the word *I;* make it *you,* if possible ("You were so kind to . . . ," "You might be interested . . . ," etc.). Keep your recipient in the forefront because—let's face it—that's what will hold the reader's interest. Not: "I just thought I'd drop you a note to say that I really enjoyed my time as your guest last week." But instead: "What a wonderful host you were last week."
- ***Say something that matters.*** Make your message pointed but substantive—not just airy filler. Not: "I trust this finds you prospering in business, thriving in your personal life, and continuing to seek the wisdom that will bring lasting satisfaction in all your dealings." But instead: "I hope you and your family and friends all dodged the fires last week in Maniton Springs—which sounded devastating."
- ***Avoid hedging and equivocating.*** Not: "It is with regret that we acknowledge that we do not appear at this time to be in a position to extend an offer of employment." But instead: "We're sorry to say that we aren't now hiring."

NOT THIS:	BUT THIS:
Enclosed please find . . .	Here are . . .; Enclosed are . . .
As per your request . . .	As you requested . . .
We are in receipt of . . .	We've received . . .
We shall advise you . . .	We'll let you know . . .
As per your letter . . .	As your letter notes . . .
We have your order and will transmit same . . .	We'll forward your order promptly . . .
We take pleasure . . .	We're glad . . .
Due to the fact that . . .	Because . . .
At an early date . . .	Soon . . .
In respect of the matter of . . .	Regarding . . .

People often overwrite their letters—studding their language with stiff, wordy expressions—when they're uncomfortable with the message. Consider the difference between the two examples that follow. The first letter is a greeting to customers from a hotel manager; the second is my revision.

NOT THIS:

Dear Valued Guest:

Welcome to the Milford Hotel Santa Clara. We are delighted that you have selected our hotel during the time when you will be here in the Silicon Valley area. Our staff is ready to assist you in any way and ensure that your stay here is an enjoyable and excellent one in every way.

During your time here at the Milford Hotel Santa Clara, we would like to inform you that the hotel is installing new toilet facilities in all guest rooms. This project will begin on Tuesday, May 8 until Tuesday, May 29. The project engineers will begin at 9:00 a.m. and conclude for the day at 5:30 p.m. The team of associates will begin work on the 14th floor and will work in descending order until completion. During these hours, you may see the new or old toilets in the guest room corridors during the exchange process, and we will ensure that a high level of cleanliness standards will be upheld. We think you'll soon appreciate fresh toilet seats. Should you be in your guest room during the toilet exchange and/or wish not to be disturbed, we recommend that you please utilize your Do Not Disturb sign by placing it on the handle of your guest room door.

The vending area should remain sanitary, so feel free to have a candy bar or beverage of your preference. For your convenience, there are safes located in the bottom nightstand drawer in your guest room to safely store your valuables. There may also be available to you utilization of our safe deposit boxes located at the Front Desk.

We appreciate your cooperation and understanding while we continue to improve the delivery system and appearance of our guest room product. Our goal is to minimize any inconvenience related to the toilet-exchange project. Please contact our Manager on Duty should you have any questions or concerns. Once again, please be assured of our utmost devotion to the total quality of your stay within the confines of the Milford Hotel Santa Clara. On behalf of myself and all the other management personnel and staff of employees here, we wish to reiterate our thanks for your selection and confidence that each and every factor of your stay here will be more than satisfactory.

Sincerely,

[386 words]

BUT THIS:

Dear Valued Guest:

Welcome to the Milford Hotel Santa Clara. We're delighted you're staying here, and we're ready to help make your stay both enjoyable and productive.

This month, we're renovating the bathrooms, starting with the 14th floor and working our way down. Although you may have occasion to see or hear workers (during the day), we're striving to minimize disruptions.

Always feel free to use your "Do Not Disturb" sign while you're in your room to ensure that our staff will respect your privacy. And if the renovations ever become a nuisance, please call me (extension 4505): I'll see what I can do. The renovations are but one example of our commitment to providing first-rate lodging.

Thank you again for joining us.

Sincerely,

[125 words]

The original is verbose (*guest room product*), perversely repetitious (the word *toilet* appears five times), hyperbolic (*excellent . . . in every way*), bureaucratic-sounding (*there may also be available to you utilization*), unpleasantly vivid (*you may see the new or old toilets*), and even gross (*have a candy bar* right after *you may see the new or old toilets*). It seems destined to arouse ill-feeling and to drive away customers who bother to read it. The revised version, by contrast, conveys warmth and consideration with its "you" focus.

Start fast, and say what you need to say in the simplest way you can. Think of Olympic diving: neatly in, no splash, soon out. And if you're writing on behalf of your firm, use *we.* It's much warmer and friendlier than the passive voice (*It has been decided* vs. *We have decided*) or the impersonal third person (*this organization* vs. *we*). Consider the difference:

NOT THIS:	**BUT THIS:**
The Mercantile Association of Greater Gotham is delighted to count you among its newest members. The Mercantile Association will provide not only networking opportunities but also advantageous insurance rates, concierge services, and Internet advertising to its members. If you ever confront business issues with which the Mercantile Association might be able to devote its resources, it stands ready to be of assistance.	Here at the Mercantile Association of Greater Gotham, we're delighted to count you among our newest members. We provide not only networking opportunities but also advantageous insurance rates, concierge services, and Internet advertising. If you ever confront business issues we can help with, we'll do whatever we can. Just let us know.

In the left-hand example, passive voice (*is delighted*) and repetition of the organization's name (it appears in every sentence) put distance between the writer and the reader. They make the communication sound like a commercial or promotion. But the *you*s and *we*s in the version on the right create a sense of belonging, a personal connection.

Motivate readers to act

Business letters get results when they meet readers' needs. To get people to do something, give them reasons they'll care about.

Consider one of the most challenging kinds of letters to write: a fund-raising appeal for a nonprofit group. The key is to understand why people give money to charitable organizations. Although marketers often cite seven "fundamental motivators" to explain responses—fear, guilt, exclusivity, greed, anger, salvation, and flattery—the reality is a bit more nuanced. Some combination of eight major reasons might motivate donors to send money in response to your appeal:

- They believe their gifts will make a difference.
- They believe in the value of organizations like yours.
- They will receive favorable recognition for the gift.
- They will be associated with a famous or respected person.
- They will enhance their sense of belonging to a worthy group.
- They will be able to relieve emotional burdens such as fear and guilt.

- They feel a sense of duty.
- They will receive tax benefits.

Certain principles follow from these reasons for giving. A successful fund-raising letter must (1) appeal directly from one person to another; (2) depict an opportunity for the recipient to satisfy personal needs by supporting a worthwhile aim; and (3) prompt the recipient to take a specific, decisive action. (These principles apply to other types of business letters as well.)

Note how all this theory plays out in an actual fund-raising letter:

> Dear Marion:
>
> May I count you in as a table sponsor at the Annual Dinner of the Tascosa Children's Home of North Texas? Your sponsorship will pay a month's room and board for one of the 50 orphaned teenagers that we care for.
>
> The event will be held at 6:00 p.m. on July 1 at Snowdon Country Club, and the emcee will be the nationally syndicated television host Spooner Hudson—our longtime national spokesperson. Celebrity chef Margrit Lafleur promises to serve up one of his memorable dinners, and the wines will be personally selected by master sommelier Peter Brunswick. Most excitingly, two mystery guests from Beverly Hills will be there that evening—among the best-known philanthropists in the world.
>
> As a table sponsor, you'll be credited as one of our Patron Angels—and, believe me, the tangible gratitude

of our kids will bring you the lasting satisfaction that you have vastly improved their lives and well-being. Our kids are reachable and teachable, but only through the generosity of our community's philanthropic leaders.

Many people, of course, can't help us in our mission. We count on our Patron Angels. I hope you'll spend a few minutes browsing through the Home's brochure (enclosed) and that you'll fill out the card committing to fill ten seats at your table (a $1,500 tax-deductible gift).

I look forward to hearing from you soon.

Sincerely,

Now look again at the bulleted list that precedes the letter to Marion (our fictitious recipient): The writer deals with every item on the list. With a letter like that, you can hope to elicit prompt action from an acceptable percentage of recipients.

Ease into bad news

If you have a rejection to deliver in your letter, sandwich it between happier elements. Don't start with a direct "no." Your readers can bear disappointment more easily if you begin on a genuine positive note and then explain the reason for the negative decision. They'll also be more likely to grant your wishes—make a purchase, sign up for your webinar, renew a membership—despite your denying theirs.

NOT THIS:	BUT THIS:
We regret to inform you that we cannot supply the 500 copies of *Negotiate It Now!* at the 60% discount that you have requested. No one—not even one of our authors, and not even the biggest bookselling chains—receives such a hefty discount. If you would care to resubmit your order at the more modest figure of 30%, we will gladly consider the order at that time. But I can offer no guarantees.	How rewarding to hear that you intend to use *Negotiate It Now!* as part of your business summit. You've chosen the best book on the subject, and we'd be delighted to supply it. Although you've requested a 60% discount off list price, the most we can offer is 30%. That's the largest discount available to anyone, and we're happy to extend it to you with a purchase of 500 copies.

Recipients of bad news will probably be unhappy no matter what. But to some extent you can control just how unhappy they'll be. Some tips:

- Adopt the reader's perspective—and be your best self. If your correspondent is rude, be polite; if anxious, be sympathetic; if confused, be lucid; if stubborn, be patient; if helpful, show gratitude; if accusatory, be reasonable and just in admitting any faults.
- Answer questions directly.
- Don't overexplain. Say only as much as necessary to get your point across.
- Put things in the simplest possible terms—never use "insider talk" or bizspeak.
- Use the voice of a thoughtful human being, not a robot.

Even if your letter grants a benefit or request, it may irk the recipient if it does so in a way that puzzles, sounds grudging, or seems indifferent to the reader's predicament.

NOT THIS:	**BUT THIS:**
Joan— In response to your request for a travel subsidy to the conference where your award will be given, Jonathan has reminded me of our current discretionary-spending freeze. He has decided, however, to make an exception in this instance so long as your flight is no more than $400 and you stick to a $50 per diem. Please submit your fully documented expenses upon your return. Sincerely, Rebekah	Joan— Congratulations on your Spivey Award! We're delighted for you. Jonathan hastened to tell me that despite our current discretionary-spending freeze, he wants to support your travel to accept your award. We can manage a $400 flight reimbursement and a $50 per diem for on-the-ground expenses. You'll be a great company representative, I know, and I only wish I could be there myself to see you honored. Sincerely, Rebekah
Brandy— At this time you have now used up all your available sick-leave days and vacation days for the year. A sister-in-law does not qualify for the closeness of relation required for an employee to be eligible for compensated bereavement leave, so you will be docked for any days you choose to be absent next week around the time of the funeral. I'm afraid that policy is simply inflexible, and I checked with Jane to confirm this. Sincerely, Pamela	Brandy— Once again I want to extend my condolences for your family's loss. Take the time you need next week to be with your family. I'm sorry to report that the days will be uncompensated, according to our policies for bereavement leave, but I hope you'll call on me if I can do anything else for you in this time of need. Jane joins me in sending our heartfelt sympathies. Sincerely, Pamela

ENCLOSED PLEASE FIND

See what business-writing authors have long said about this wooden phrase and others like it:

Richard Grant White (1880): "[*Please find enclosed:*] A more ridiculous use of words, it seems to me, there could not be."

Sherwin Cody (1908): "All stereotyped words [that] are not used in talking should be avoided in letter writing. There is an idea that a certain peculiar commercial jargon is appropriate in business letters. The fact is, nothing injures business more than this system of words found only in business letters. The test of a word or phrase or method of expression should be, 'Is it what I would say to my customer if I were talking to him instead of writing to him?'"

Wallace E. Bartholomew & Floyd Hurlbut (1924): "*Inclosed herewith please find. Inclosed* and *herewith* mean the same thing. How foolish to tell your reader twice exactly where the check is, and then to suggest that he look around to see if he can find it anywhere. Say, 'We are inclosing our check for $25.50.'"

A. Charles Babenroth (1942): "*Enclosed please find.* Needless and faulty phraseology. The word *please* has little meaning in this instance, and the word *find* is improperly used. POOR: Enclosed please find sample of our #1939 black elastic ribbon. BETTER: We are enclosing (or We enclose) a sample of our #1939 black elastic ribbon."

***L. E. Frailey (1965)*:** "So much for the worn-out, hackneyed expressions [*enclosed herewith, enclosed please find, herewith please find*] so often seen in business letters—whiskers, rubber-stamps, chestnuts, call them what you please. They are sleeping pills [that] defeat the aim of making every letter a warm, personal contact with the reader."

***Gerald J. Alred, Charles T. Brusaw, & Walter E. Oliu (1993)*:** "Using unnecessarily formal words (such as *herewith*) and outdated phrases (such as *please find enclosed*) is another cause of affectation."

***Kelly Cannon (2004)*:** "[I]n any business letter, certain principles are universal. 'Inure to the benefit of' is four words too long, 'enclosed please find' sounds pompous and silly, and 'I am writing this letter to inform you that . . .' is a thoughtless statement of the obvious."

Don't write in anger

Be kind and diplomatic, and say *please* and *thank you.* Courtesy is necessary to all business transactions—even letters of complaint. Omit it, and you'll be dismissed as a crank. You can be courteous while still being direct.

NOT THIS:	BUT THIS:
We are astonished at your complaint. The brochures that we printed were exactly as you specified. You okayed the sample paper, the typesetting, and the proofreading (we gave you an extra three hours). You chose the hot-pink borders with the fine-screen halftones in the body type against our advice. You insisted on drop-shipping by the 18th, and as you know, a rushed job does not allow for first-rate press work. Moreover, we quoted you a bargain-basement price. Under the circumstances we believe that any unbiased observer would say that we performed remarkably well under the impossible conditions you imposed.	We agree with you that the brochures did not match the high standards you have a right to expect from us. But we believed, in this instance, that you considered the color quality less crucial than a low price and a quick turnaround. So we pushed the work through production in three days' less time than we usually require. We advised against your using hot-pink borders and fine-screen halftones on the grade of paper you chose. Still, we exercised some ingenuity to achieve better results than are ordinarily possible. I mention this not to avoid responsibility but merely to suggest that we did the best that could be done under difficult circumstances. If you'll allow us a few more days next time, as you ordinarily do, the results will be better.

As you can see, a combative, superior tone irritates and alienates the reader—and probably loses a customer. A more diplomatic approach still gets the point across (rush jobs always take a hit on quality), but without souring the relationship.

When you receive unreasonable letters, don't ever respond in kind. That just starts a negative chain reaction. Approach complaints with a dedication to first-rate service. Write with the same warmth and friendliness you'd use in face-to-face conversations. If you or your company made a mistake, avoid the temptation to ignore it, cover it up, or shift the blame. Instead of deceiving readers, you'll provoke more ire. When you blunder, admit error and say what you've done (or will be doing) to correct it. Stress the desire to improve service.

Recap

- Keep your language simple, personal, and direct. Avoid canned phrases that add little but pomposity and verbiage to your letter.
- Motivate your readers to act on your letter by giving them reasons that matter to them.
- When conveying bad news, soften the blow by opening on a positive note. Follow up by explaining the reason for the unfavorable outcome—without overexplaining.
- Consider the reader: Be polite, sympathetic, and professional.
- Remain courteous and diplomatic. Accept responsibility for any mistakes you may have made.

Chapter 20
Memos and Reports

Memos and reports are often used to get people up to speed on an issue, to induce action, or both. So make it immediately clear in each element—your title, summary, body, and conclusion—what you want readers to learn about or do.

Pick a short, clear title

Whether you're writing a memo's subject line or a report title, choose concise, sure-footed language that says exactly what the document is about.

NOT THIS:	BUT THIS:
Subject: Siegelson	Subject: Approval of Siegelson Acquisition
Subject: Settlement	Subject: Why We Should Reject Frost's Settlement Offer
Subject: Print Run	Subject: Ginsburg Autobiography Print Run

The titles on the left hint at the topics covered but don't let readers know what they're supposed to do with the information. Those on the right are more pointed (without being wordy): The first and third titles promise status updates; the second asks readers to follow a recommendation.

Summarize key specifics up front

Figure out how many main issues you're addressing—preferably no more than three (see chapter 4)—and then for each one state: (1) the issue in a way that *anyone* can understand, (2) your solution, and (3) the reason for your solution. Here's an example:

Summary

Issue: Arnold Paper Supply has consistently failed to meet our deadlines for delivery of multicolor, printed cardstock.

Proposed Solution: Switch to National Paper and Plastics Company, which has a higher fixed fee.

Reason: Though National Paper and Plastics Company has a higher rate per delivery, its turnaround is quicker. This will increase efficiency in the warehouse, allow us to fill more orders, and help us to establish goodwill with retailers who have been angry with us for not meeting their deadlines.

By sharing everything important at the beginning of the document, you'll end up repeating yourself—but in a way that's reinforcing, not redundant. Readers will get a quick orientation with your very short version up front;

the fully elaborated version in the body will unpack each point, providing details and data for support. I recommend going back and forth between the summary and the body when writing your first draft: Start by stating the problem and offering your best shot at the answer in your summary. As you do more work on the body of the memo or report, you'll go back and refine the problem and the answer.

Write your summary for three types of readers:

- A primary audience of one or more executives interested only in a quick status update, your findings and conclusions about a problem, or your recommendations.
- A line of readers who may be called in (with or without your knowledge) to assess the soundness of your document, judging its merits according to their own fact-checking and critical analysis.
- Future readers (including those in the first category two years from now) who will be required to quarry information from your document some time after you've written it. (After all, memos and reports are rarely acted on quickly: They may be laid aside for weeks or months or even years before anyone has the resources—or a mandate—to act.)

All three types of readers have a legitimate claim to your attention. More important, you need to win them all over if you want your recommendations to go anywhere.

Even if someone else has assigned you the question you're exploring, you must define it in your summary.

WHEN WRITING A REPORT . . .

- Make sure you understand why you're writing and what you're reporting on.
- Do your best, in light of your background knowledge and initial research, to write a summary that concisely states the problem, your solution, and why your solution will work or why it's preferable to alternatives.
- Discern sources of relevant information.
- From those sources, gather all the data and explanations that you can.
- Synthesize relevant observations and inferences and throw out the rest.
- Put your findings into report form.
- Revise your summary to match your body text.

You, the writer, are in the best position to limit its scope: The person who did the assigning may not know enough about the problem to raise the right question—or to understand that it actually contains three subquestions.

In fact, you won't know these things until you do your research, which may involve digging up data that reveal where the problem lurks, reading about how other organizations have tried to solve it, talking with people who have discovered some helpful workarounds, and so on.

You should do enough research to understand the problem. *Then* you state the problem so clearly that anyone could understand why it's worth solving.

If you're making a recommendation, say (1) what needs to be done, (2) who should do it, (3) when and where it should be done, (4) why it should be done, and (5) how it should be done.

A brief marketing report might look like this:

Marketing Strategy for Skinny Mini Line of Chocolates

Summary

Issue: Within the last fiscal year, Pantheon Chocolate's sales have dropped from $13,320,000 to $10,730,000, but its market share remains unchanged at 37%.

Proposed Solution: Increase promotion of the Skinny Mini line of chocolates. These chocolates contain less sugar and fat than the regular line.

Reason: Health-conscious consumers want low-calorie options but don't want to sacrifice full flavor. The Skinny Mini chocolates have fewer calories than Pantheon's regular chocolates but the same flavor.

Consumers are buying more "healthy alternative" chocolates

Because consumers increasingly regard sugar and fat as unhealthy, they are not buying as much high-end gourmet chocolate as they were a year ago. This has led to a decline in sales for all high-end chocolate makers, including Pantheon. But for candies marketed as "healthy alternatives" with less sugar and fat and fewer calories, sales have increased 42% in the same period. Marketing studies show that consumers of "healthy alternative" candies are most attracted to low-calorie chocolates that are packaged in specific-calorie portions rather than by weight.

These consumers also complain that low-calorie candies lack the rich flavor that they are used to, and they are willing to pay more for quality. Pantheon already produces a line of low-calorie gourmet chocolates, Skinny Minis, that have fewer calories than Pantheon's regular candies but the same flavor. They're currently sold by the pound or in gift boxes in high-end chocolate boutiques and as elegantly wrapped bars in coffee shops.

Recommendations

- To reach more health-conscious consumers, Pantheon should package Skinny Mini chocolates in a variety of portion-controlled sizes and make them available in health-food stores and supermarkets as well as the chocolate and coffee shops.
- The marketing campaign should stress the controlled portion and limited calories of each Skinny Mini bar or gift box, and the packaging should boldly display the low calorie count.

Recap

- Choose a concise title or subject line that tells readers what topics the memo or report covers and what they should do about it (or why they should care).

- Begin your document by addressing your main points and outlining the issue, your solution, and the reason for it.
- Work from this summary when elaborating the body of your first draft.
- Modify the summary as you go to ensure that it accurately reflects what's in the body.

Chapter 21
Performance Appraisals

Writing performance appraisals, sometimes called employee reviews, needn't be a dreaded responsibility. As long as you have gathered your facts in advance—reviewed the notes you've taken throughout the year, asked others for feedback on the people you supervise, and carefully read people's self-assessments—the drafting isn't onerous if you have an ample evaluative vocabulary. I've written this chapter so you'll have some helpful phrases at the ready.

The sample phrases that follow address seven aspects of work: attitude, efficiency, human relations, judgment, knowledge, reliability, and communication skills. But you can adapt the wording to suit whatever qualities you'd like to focus on. Then it's a matter of pairing the phrases with specifics that support them. For example: "When we had several layoffs last June, Lauren *remained utterly calm and collected* while *demonstrating keen sensitivity* to those who lost their jobs. She [fill in whatever particular action was noteworthy]."

Attitude

Superb	• shows unwavering commitment • always gives maximal effort • is always friendly and happy to help • always brings out the best in others
Good	• shows strong commitment • usually makes a strong effort • is usually friendly and happy to help • usually brings out the best in others
Acceptable	• shows adequate commitment • makes an effort • is often friendly and happy to help • is often a positive influence on the group
Needs Improvement	• could show more commitment • doesn't always make an effort • is sometimes quarrelsome • sometimes creates tension within the group
Poor	• lacks commitment • rarely makes a real effort • is quarrelsome and sometimes even hostile • often creates tension within the group

Efficiency

Superb	• never wastes time or effort • delegates effectively • always completes tasks on time • can manage many projects at a time
Good	• rarely wastes time or effort • usually delegates appropriately • almost always completes tasks on time • can manage several projects at a time
Acceptable	• usually doesn't waste time or effort • delegates pretty well • usually completes tasks on time • can manage more than one project at a time
Needs Improvement	• sometimes wastes time and effort • tries to do too much without delegating • fails to complete tasks on time • cannot manage more than one project at a time
Poor	• often wastes time and effort • usually fails to delegate when appropriate • can't be counted on to complete tasks on time • struggles to manage even one project at a time

Human relations

Superb	• demonstrates keen sensitivity to others and an uncanny ability to understand their needs • participates actively and collegially in meetings • works exceptionally well on teams • relates to customers extremely well

Good

- usually demonstrates sensitivity to others
- participates effectively in meetings
- works effectively on teams
- relates to customers well

Acceptable

- often demonstrates sensitivity to others
- participates adequately in meetings
- gets along with fellow team members
- relates to customers competently

Needs Improvement

- does not always pick up on interpersonal cues
- sometimes wastes others' time in meetings
- is sometimes motivated more by personal goals than by team goals
- sometimes alienates customers through inattention

Poor

- rarely pays attention to others' reactions
- often wastes others' time in meetings
- does not work well on teams
- often alienates customers with impoliteness and sarcasm

Judgment

Superb

- makes excellent choices and informed decisions
- remains utterly calm and collected even in times of crisis
- knows precisely which problems need immediate attention and which ones can wait
- behaves professionally and appropriately in every situation

Good

- makes sound choices and reasonable decisions
- remains relatively calm and collected even in times of crisis
- generally knows which problems need immediate attention and which ones can wait
- behaves professionally and appropriately

Acceptable

- generally makes sound choices and informed decisions
- remains mostly calm and collected except in times of crisis
- does a pretty good job distinguishing between problems that need immediate attention and those that can wait
- generally behaves professionally and appropriately

Needs Improvement

- sometimes makes poor choices and ill-informed decisions
- sometimes lacks the calm and collected demeanor required in high-pressure circumstances
- often doesn't distinguish between problems that need immediate attention and those that can wait
- sometimes behaves unprofessionally and inappropriately

Judgment (*continued*)

Poor	• often makes poor choices and ill-informed decisions • often lacks the calm and collected demeanor required in high-pressure circumstances • typically fails to distinguish between problems that need immediate attention and those that can wait • often behaves unprofessionally and inappropriately

Knowledge

Superb	• is exceptionally well informed about all aspects of the job • demonstrates extraordinarily comprehensive knowledge • skillfully handles complex assignments without supervision • has a comprehensive knowledge of the industry
Good	• is well informed about key aspects of the job • demonstrates thorough knowledge • can handle complex assignments with some supervision • has strong knowledge of the industry
Acceptable	• understands the job • demonstrates adequate knowledge • can handle moderately complex assignments with supervision • has an acceptable degree of knowledge of the industry
Needs Improvement	• doesn't fully understand the job • demonstrates less than satisfactory knowledge • sometimes mishandles assignments of moderate complexity, even with supervision • has insufficient knowledge of the industry
Poor	• is ill-informed about many aspects of the job • demonstrates inadequate knowledge • mishandles basic assignments • has little knowledge of the industry

Reliability

Superb	• always meets deadlines • is unfailingly dependable • achieves excellent results in urgent situations • always delivers on promises
Good	• meets deadlines • is highly dependable • achieves good results in urgent situations • almost always delivers on promises
Acceptable	• meets most deadlines • is dependable • achieves acceptable results in urgent situations • delivers pretty consistently on promises

Needs Improvement	• sometimes fails to meet important deadlines • is sometimes undependable • sometimes fails to achieve acceptable results in urgent situations • sometimes fails to deliver on promises
Poor	• often fails to meet important deadlines • is rarely dependable • often fails to achieve acceptable results in urgent situations • can't be counted on to deliver on promises

Communication skills

Superb	• writes and speaks with remarkable clarity • never gets bogged down in unnecessary details • has superior communication skills in person and over the phone • develops and delivers imaginative, clear, and concise presentations
Good	• writes and speaks clearly • rarely gets bogged down in unnecessary details • has sound communication skills in person and over the phone • develops and delivers clear, concise presentations
Acceptable	• generally writes and speaks clearly • usually avoids getting bogged down in unnecessary details • has adequate communication skills in person and over the phone • develops and delivers acceptable presentations
Needs Improvement	• sometimes writes and speaks unclearly and with undue complexity • sometimes gets bogged down in unnecessary details • sometimes struggles to communicate in person and over the phone • develops and delivers presentations in need of further work and polish
Poor	• writes and speaks unclearly and with undue complexity • gets bogged down in unnecessary details • fails to communicate effectively in person and over the phone • develops and delivers presentations that ramble and lack clarity

Recap

- Prepare by gathering your facts in advance: Keep performance notes throughout the year and review them before writing. Ask other colleagues for feedback on those you're evaluating. Carefully review the employees' self-assessments.
- Use the sample phrases provided here to help articulate your impressions.
- Always pair your general statements with specific examples that support them.

Appendix A
A Checklist for the Four Stages of Writing

Madman

- ☐ Consider why you're writing: What's moved you to write? What's the assignment? What do you hope to achieve?
- ☐ Think about who your readers are and what they need to know.
- ☐ Figure out how much time you have, and work out a rough schedule for gathering ideas and material, outlining, preparing a draft, and revising.
- ☐ Research with imagination and gusto. Take notes on relevant information.
- ☐ Push yourself to be creative. Don't be content with obvious ideas that just anyone would think of.

Architect

- ☐ Jot down your three main points in complete sentences—with as much specificity as you can.
- ☐ Consider the best order of the three points and reorganize them if necessary.
- ☐ Decide how to open and conclude the document.
- ☐ Think about what visual aids might be helpful in conveying your ideas.

Carpenter

- ☐ If possible, turn away from all distractions. Silence your phone and your computer alerts, and find an hour or so of solitude. You'll be writing.
- ☐ Use your three-point outline as a guide.
- ☐ Start writing paragraphs that support the point you find easiest to start with—then move to the other points.
- ☐ Write swiftly without stopping to edit or polish.
- ☐ Try to write a full section in one sitting. If you must get up in the middle of a section, start the next sentence with a few words and then leave. (When you come back, you'll find it easier to resume a half-completed sentence than to start a new one.)

Judge

- ☐ Immediately after completing your draft, read it through with the idea of amplifying ideas here and there.
- ☐ Then let it cool off—overnight, if you can, or for a few minutes if you're working under an urgent deadline.
- ☐ When you return to your draft, consider it from the audience's perspective. Will it be clear to everyone who looks at it, or does it require inside knowledge? Is it concise, or does it waste words and time?
- ☐ Identify the draft's two biggest flaws and try to fix them.
- ☐ Ask yourself:
    - Is anything essential missing?
    - Are important points stressed?
    - Is the meaning of each sentence clear and accurate?
    - Are my transitions smooth?
    - What can I trim without sacrificing important content?
    - Are there any vague passages I can sharpen with specific facts?
    - Are there boring passages I can word more vividly?
    - Can I improve the phrasing?
    - Can I improve the punctuation?
    - Are there any typos?

Appendix B

A Dozen Grammatical Rules You Absolutely Need to Know

1. **It is perfectly acceptable to start a sentence with *And* or *But*.**

   The single most important element in fluid writing is the use of effective transitions between sentences and paragraphs. And no transition is more effective than the plain single-syllable words *and* and *but.*

   The notion that it's ungrammatical to start a sentence with a conjunction has long been ignored by the best writers and debunked by reputable grammarians. Look at the op-ed page of any major newspaper or scan through some pages of any well-edited magazine and you'll see plenty of examples. Why? Because conjunctions are excellent transition tools, signaling how the sentence to follow fits in with what came before—and because they're short, sharp, and fleet. *And* and *but* are usually more effective than clunky conjunctive adverbs such as *additionally* and *however,* which add syllables and demand a comma after them.

2. **It is perfectly acceptable to end a sentence with a preposition.**
The "rule" that you should not end a sentence with a preposition is a misbegotten notion based on Latin syntax and expounded by a few (a very few) 19th-century writers. Grammarians have long since dismissed it as ill-founded and unnecessary.

    Often a sentence that ends with a preposition sounds far more natural than the same sentence forced into avoiding the terminal preposition. Consider: *What will the new product be used for?* versus *For what purpose will the new product be used?*

    That said, a strong sentence should end forcefully because the end of a sentence is the most emphatic position. A preposition is rarely a powerful sentence-ender, but it is not an ungrammatical one.

3. **The adverb corresponding to the adjective *good* is *well*.**
When describing performance, manner, action, and the like, use the adverb *well* <The intern

works well under pressure> <The research and development stage is going well> <We wish them well in the future>. Though becoming more widespread, the adverbial use of *good* is nonstandard English <The vice presidents *worked good as a team> <The new water pump *is running good>. The question whether to use *good* or *well* frequently arises when someone asks "How are you doing?" The best answer—assuming a positive response—is "I'm doing well" (or "I'm fine, thank you"). Saying "I'm good" is common but unrefined. The response "I'm *doing good" is substandard because *good* is there being used as an adverb. An exception to the rule against using *good* as an adverb applies with certain set phrases <a good many more> <did it but good>.

4. **The subject of the sentence determines the number of the verb.**

A subject and its verb must both be either singular or plural. Grammar Girl says so. (*Grammar Girl* and *says* are both singular.) All grammarians say so. (*Grammarians* and *say* are both plural.) The rule seems so elementary as to be trivial. But a lot can go wrong. A prepositional phrase modifying the subject is a common source of trouble: Should *an oversupply of foreign imports* take a singular or plural verb? The answer is singular, to match the subject *oversupply.* Although compound subjects generally take plural verbs, sometimes a subject really expresses a single (and singular) idea <The company's bread and butter is still shipping>. The subject, *bread and butter,* is plural in form but singular in sense, so it takes the singular verb *is.*

There (in its use as a subject stand-in, as in *There is another way*) presents a special problem, one that some authorities call the most common grammatical error today. In inverted sentences, the true subject follows the verb <There go our fourth-quarter profits>. The subject *profits* is after the verb *go.* Yet people seem to want singular verbs with *there* regardless of what follows, and errors result <*There is still market capacity and established competition to be considered>. The compound subject *capacity and competition* should take the plural verb *are,* not the singular verb *is.*

Illusory compounds can also cause trouble. These occur with constructions such as *together with, as well as,* and the like, none of which forms a plural. <The board, along with the president and CFO, endorses the stock split>. The subject is the singular *board,* which takes the singular verb *endorses.*

5. **Both *either* and *neither*, as subjects, take singular verbs.**

Beware of distractions caused by prepositional phrases containing plural objects: The subject—*either* or *neither*—is still singular <Either of the marketing plans *involves* [not *involve*] capital investment> <Neither of our expansion options *provides* [not *provide*] a total solution>.

6. **With *neither/nor* and *either/or* in the subject position, the second element controls the number of the verb.**
   When the correlative conjunctions *either/or* or *neither/nor* frame alternatives in the singular, the verb is singular <Either phone or fax *is* acceptable for your response>. When the alternatives are plural, the verb is plural <Neither our accountants nor our lawyers *are* concerned about the merger>. But when one element is singular and the other is plural, match the verb to the second element <Neither the regional managers nor the vice-president for sales *likes* [not *like*] the proposed campaign's theme> <Either the home office or the branch managers *are* [not *is*] largely responsible for employee morale>.

7. **A flat adverb like *thus* or *doubtless* takes no *-ly* ending.**
   Most adverbs are formed by adding the *-ly* suffix to adjectives (*large* makes *largely, quick* makes *quickly*) or changing the *-able* suffix to *-ably* (*amicable* makes *amicably, capable* makes *capably*). But the English language also contains a fair number of adverbs that do not

end in *-ly* (such as *fast, ill,* and *seldom*). With these, it is unnecessary—and unidiomatic—to add the suffix *-ly*. The two most common examples are **doubtlessly* and **thusly*.

8. **The words *however, therefore,* and *otherwise* cannot join independent clauses without additional punctuation.**
   An independent clause (1) contains a subject and a verb and (2) expresses a complete thought. It can stand alone as a sentence, or it can be connected with another clause by a comma and a conjunction (such as *and, but, or*) <The new advertising campaign is ready, but the CEO has yet to approve it>. When two independent clauses are joined with a conjunctive adverb like *however*, a semicolon must go in front of the connector and a comma after <Mr. Bingham can't attend the meeting; however, he hopes to call before we adjourn>. Omitting the semicolon or replacing it with a comma creates what is known as a "comma splice" <*We were supposed to arrive at 4:00 p.m., however, we didn't arrive until 5:00>.

9. **With a verb phrase, the adverb usually goes after the first auxiliary verb.**
   Writing authorities have long agreed that midphrase is the strongest and most natural place for an adverb <Industry experts *have long agreed* on the product's effectiveness>. The alternatives are awkward <Industry experts

long have agreed on the product's effectiveness> or nonsensical <Industry experts *have agreed long* on the product's effectiveness>. Resistance to this guidance may be due to the old superstition that it's ungrammatical to split an infinitive (it isn't), since that is one type of split verb <We expect the new product line and expanded territory *to almost double* our sales in the next two years>.

When the phrase has more than one auxiliary verb, the most natural placement is usually after the first one (as in *has long been assumed*).

10. **Relative pronouns (*that, which,* and *who*) must appear alongside their antecedents.**

A relative pronoun (*that, which, who, whom,* and various forms with the *-ever* suffix) serves one of two purposes. First, it can link a dependent clause to an independent one <Whoever wants to participate is welcome>. The dependent clause (*whoever wants to participate*) serves as the subject of the main clause. Second, it can join a clause with its antecedent <Those who want to participate are welcome>. Here, the dependent clause (*who want to participate*) adds crucial information about its antecedent, *those.*

The second type of relative pronoun should be close to its antecedent—preferably immediately after it. The link must be clear because trouble can occur when the reference becomes uncertain <*Please discuss the customer-service position in the accounting department that is being eliminated>. Which is being eliminated, the position or the department? Restating the sentence clarifies it <Please discuss the customer-service position that is being eliminated in the accounting department>. The relative pronoun *that* immediately follows its antecedent, *customer-service position.*

11. **An appositive is set off by commas when it is not essential to the sentence (when it is nonrestrictive), but is not set off by commas when it is essential (restrictive).**

An appositive is a noun or noun phrase that follows another noun (or pronoun) and identifies or depicts it more fully <My colleague Pat agrees> <The customer, a tall man in an oversized suit, left his keys on the counter>.

In the first example, the appositive *Pat* is not set off by commas from the rest of the sentence. In the second, *a tall man in an oversized suit* is set off. The reason is that appositives, like relative clauses (those introduced by *which, who,* and *whom*), may or may not be essential to the meaning of the sentence. *Pat,* in the first sentence, is essential—it specifies which colleague (presumably out of several) is being referred to. In the second sentence, the appositive merely adds description. We could also say that *Pat,* in the first sentence, defines or restricts its referent, *colleague,* while the appositive in the second sense is indefinite or nonrestrictive. Current stylebooks use the terms *restrictive* and *nonrestrictive* to label these qualities.

Appositives may also be set off by em-dashes (typically for emphasis) or parentheses (typically for deemphasis) instead of commas.

12. Correlative conjunctions (those used in pairs) require parallel phrasing.

Correlative conjunctions (such as *both . . . and, neither . . . nor,* and *not only . . . but also*) work in pairs, joining related constructions that match in syntax. Each conjunction should immediately precede the part of speech it describes. Parallelism is rarely a problem with simple nouns <neither time nor money>, but it becomes tricky with phrases and clauses, as in the erroneous phrasing **We not only raised our regional market share but also our profit margin,* which should read: *We raised not only our regional market share but also our profit margin.* The verb *raised* must be outside the first correlative conjunction (*not only*) to apply to both possessive phrases (*our regional market share* and *our profit margin*).

Appendix C

A Dozen Punctuation Rules You Absolutely Need to Know

1. **Hyphenate your phrasal adjectives.**

   A *small-business incentive* is different from a *small business incentive.* A *limited-liability clause* is different from a *limited liability clause.* When two or more words as a unit modify a noun, they must be hyphenated (unless certain exceptions apply). So a hotel's door sign advising the staff not to disturb the guests would be a *do-not-disturb sign.* A company that is 25 years old is a *25-year-old company.*

   There are some exceptions: (1) Don't hyphenate simple phrases formed by an *-ly* adverb and a past-participial adjective <a greatly

exaggerated claim>. (2) Don't hyphenate phrases formed with proper nouns <New Zealand exports> or foreign words <a post facto rationalization>. (3) Generally, don't hyphenate phrasal adjectives used after the noun they modify <a job well done>, but there are exceptions based solely on conventions of usage <our HR manager is risk-averse by nature> <the information is time-sensitive>.

2. **Use a comma before *and* or *or* when listing three or more items.**

   Although simple series *<red, white, and blue>* might not require the so-called serial comma before the conjunction to be perfectly clear, clarity fades fast as series become longer and more complex <We hope to boost sales in the target area, to build the company's name-recognition statewide and beyond, and to attract investors for possible franchise opportunities>. So what is the rule?

   The Chicago Manual of Style and other authorities on professional, technical, and scholarly writing almost universally endorse using the serial comma in *all* series for one good reason: It is sometimes wrong (ambiguous or worse) to omit it, but never wrong to include it.

3. **Don't use a comma to separate two compound predicates. Do use punctuation—usually a comma but a semicolon if needed for clarity—to separate a series of three or more compound predicates.**

When two predicates share the same subject, it's common not to repeat the subject. If the second clause repeats the subject, then the comma is proper before the conjunction <I stopped by yesterday, and I will call today>. But if the subject isn't repeated (is shared by both predicates), there should be no comma before the conjunction <I stopped by yesterday and will call today>. When three or more such clauses are combined (sharing the same subject), the predicates become a series and do require at least a comma to separate them <I wrote him yesterday, stopped by yesterday, and will call today>.

When one or more of the parts in the series contain commas, use semicolons instead to separate the predicates <I wrote him last week; I stopped by yesterday with the paperwork, the deposit check, and the keys; and I will call him today>. The same principle holds for a compound predicate <I wrote him last week; stopped by yesterday with the paperwork, the deposit check, and the keys; and will call him today>.

4. **Don't use an apostrophe to form plural nouns.** The use of apostrophes to form plurals (rather than possessives or contractions) is almost always incorrect. Most proper nouns take a simple *-s,* while those ending in *-s, -x, -z,* and sibilant *-ch* or *-sh* take *-es*. The exceptions to the no-apostrophe rule are for lowercase

letters <Mind your p's and q's> and capital letters when an apostrophe might prevent a miscue <all A's on the audit report>. Don't use apostrophes to pluralize numbers or capitalized abbreviations without periods <ATMs became ubiquitous in the 1990s>. The usual way to pluralize words and letters is to italicize the word or letter and append *-s* in roman type <Please delete the first two *or*s in the sentence>.

The incorrect use of apostrophes is especially common when pluralizing names. Mr. and Mrs. Smith are *the Smiths,* not **the Smith's* (or **the Smiths'*). Mr. and Mrs. Stevens are *the Stevenses* (not **the Steven's* or **the Stevens'*).

5. **Don't separate the grammatical subject from the verb, unless there's a set-off intervening phrase.** As a rule, words and phrases that *go* together should *be* together, not unduly separated. So an appositive, for example, is next to the noun or pronoun it elaborates <Maeve Peterson, the new CEO, is . . .> and a pronoun should not be so far from its antecedent as to make the connection unclear. On the same principle, the subject and verb in a sentence are best kept close together so that the sentence does not wander off on tangents.

   That's not to say that an intervening phrase or clause between the subject and verb is always wrong. It can be an effective way to modify the sense or add information <Ms. Peterson, whose leadership at McLaughlin Enterprises has been credited with that firm's turnaround, will take the reins here on June 1>. Although this technique adds emphasis to the modifying matter, it's often clearer to make the phrase or clause introductory so that the subject and verb remain close <Credited with turning around McLaughlin Enterprises during her four years as CEO, Ms. Peterson starts work here on June 1>.

6. **Use bullets as attention-getting devices, but don't overuse them.**

   Bullets draw the reader's eye to a list of points without signaling that they're presented in a certain order. The best lists follow these rules:

   - Set up the list with an explanatory sentence in the form of an introduction that ends with a colon.
   - Keep all the items parallel in grammatical form (all noun phrases, say, or all predicates starting with verbs) and somewhat similar in length.
   - Present the items with a hanging indent so the bullets stand out to the left and all the lines of type align.
   - Typeset the items single-spaced, perhaps with a bit of extra spacing between items.

- Keep the bullets simple in appearance, eschewing whimsical artwork in favor of solid bullet dots about the size of a lowercase *o*.

As with any other design device aimed at signaling emphasis or attracting the reader's attention, the overuse of bulleted lists dilutes their impact.

7. **Avoid quotation marks as a way of emphasizing words.**

Quotation marks can send mixed signals. Most often they signal their traditional function: to set off a quotation. Sometimes they suggest a snide attitude <an "expert" in negotiation>, or perhaps imply that what they contain is not what it purports to be at all <Here's the "final" schedule>. They can be the equivalent of introducing the words with "so-called." Given all these different possible meanings, quotation marks are a poor choice for emphasizing words and phrases. That is traditionally the role of italic type, an unambiguous signal.

Also avoid (1) underlining, the italic font's uglier equivalent from the typewriter era; (2) overuse of boldface type, which is best reserved for titles and headings; and (3) all caps, which is irritating and hard to read if longer than a word or two.

8. **Don't hyphenate most prefixed terms.**

American English is generally averse to hyphenating its prefixes (*anteroom*, *biennial*, *deselect, proactive, quarterfinal, semisweet*). Avoid the practice of inserting a hyphen, even when it results in a doubled letter (*cooperate, reelect, misspeak*). But there are a few exceptions: (1) when it's needed to avoid a miscue or an ambiguity (*re-create, re-lease, re-sign*); (2) when the root word is a proper noun (*pre-Halloween sales*); and (3) when using certain prefixes such as *all-* (*all-inclusive*), *ex-* (*ex-partner*), and *self-* (*self-correcting*).

9. **Use a colon or a comma—never a semicolon—after a salutation.**
   Colons are standard in business correspondence <Dear Ms. Wilson:>, commas in personal letters <Dear Barbara,>. Commas may also be permissible for business letters, depending on the personal relationship between the sender and the recipient. But to use a semicolon (**Dear Mr. Jones;*) is always incorrect.

10. **Long dashes have two defensible—and valuable—uses: to frame and to emphasize.**
    First, long dashes—called *em-dashes*—frame what is basically parenthetical matter and make it stand out. Notice in the first sentence how "called *em-dashes*" stands out. It could just as easily have been set off from the rest of the sentence by commas or placed inside parentheses. But the dashes give an interruptive phrase special emphasis (while parentheses

almost beg to be skipped over). It's a strong technique that should be used but, like all effective writing devices, not overused.

Second, em-dashes are handy for short tags that sit apart from the main sentence. The em-dash replaces the colon but adds emphasis. The setoff can come at the beginning of the sentence <Customer service—it's our top priority> or at the end <No matter what the field, an able workforce starts with and continues with one thing—professional training>.

11. **Don't use a comma when writing a month and year.**

Stylebooks have long agreed that no comma should appear between the month and year <February 2012>. With the standard American format of month–day–year, do use a comma after the day <February 23, 2012>. No comma is necessary with the day–month–year format <23 February 2012>. Use a comma after the year <Groundbreaking was held February 23, 2012, in Menomonee Falls> unless the date is used adjectivally <the February 23, 2012 groundbreaking ceremonies>.

12. **For singular possessives, add *'s* even if the word ends with an -*s*, -*z*, -*x*, or -*ss*.**

This is the first rule in Strunk & White's famous book *The Elements of Style:* A singular possessive takes *'s* <Kansas's business climate> <Holtz's contract> <Xerox's patents> <the

actress's endorsement>. But note that personal pronouns and *who* have their own form without the *'s* (*mine, our, ours, your, yours, his, her, hers, its, their, theirs, whose*). Also, if the name of a corporation or other entity is formed from a plural word, add only the apostrophe <United Airlines' quarterly report> <The United Arab Emirates' capital is Abu Dhabi>.

When forming a plural possessive, use the word's standard plural form and add an apostrophe to the final *-s* <caterers' fees> <the bosses' offices>. An exception applies to plural words that don't end in *-s:* they follow the same rule as singular possessives <a line of children's clothing> <the alumnae's reunion>.

Appendix D
Common Usage Gaffes

In this top-20 list of usage points that distinguish sloppy from refined language, an asterisk precedes erroneous words and phrases.

NOT THIS:	BUT THIS:
I *feel badly about the oversight.	I feel bad about the oversight.
I'm *feeling very well about the sales figures.	I feel good (contented). I feel well (healthy).
They're *doing good.	They're doing well.
Just *between you and I.	Just between you and me.
He expected *Helen and I to help him.	He expected Helen and me to help him.
She *could care less.	She couldn't care less.
He's *laying down on the couch.	He's lying down on the couch.
*Where are you at?	Where are you?
*If I would have been there	If I had been there . . . .

NOT THIS:	BUT THIS:
She serves on the board; *as such, she has fiduciary duties.	She's a board member; as such, she has fiduciary duties.
The letter was sent *on accident.	The letter was sent by accident.
I *wish he was faster.	I wish he were faster.
I *could of done it.	I could have done it.
*in regards to	in regard to, or regarding
*less items	fewer items
He was *undoubtably guilty.	He was undoubtedly guilty.
*preventative	preventive
*There's lots of reasons.	There are lots of reasons.
*as best as she can	as best she can
*irregardless	regardless, or irrespective

For more on usage, see Appendix F.

Appendix E
Some Dos and Don'ts of Business-Writing Etiquette

Dos:

1. Proofread all documents before sending them out to make sure the spelling and grammar are correct.

2. Double-check that the recipient's name is spelled correctly and that the form of address is proper (Ms., Mrs., Miss, Mr., Dr., Judge, Justice, Honorable, etc.). Double-check the envelope, too, if there is one.

3. Sign business letters with your full name unless you're friends with the recipient. If the salutation is "Dear Mr. Smith," sign your full name; if it's "Dear George," sign your first name only.

4. Sign your letters with an ink pen and not with a stamp of your signature.
5. Always include your contact information so that the recipient will know how to respond to you.
6. If you're sending a handwritten note to a business contact or friend, use a stamp to mail the letter rather than meter-stamping the envelope.
7. Before sending an e-mail, make sure that you have (a) included everyone you need in the address block and (b) incorporated any attachments you refer to in the e-mail.
8. Use white space effectively so that the document reads well and is not a strain on people's eyes. Create generous margins, leave spaces between paragraphs, break up text with subheads if appropriate, and indent appropriately.
9. Date your communications (except e-mails, which will date themselves) so that they give the reader a reference time.
10. Write distinctive thank-you notes if you're writing them to several people in the same office. It's counterproductive if recipients compare their notes and realize you mass-produced them.

Don'ts:

1. Don't use all caps. It amounts to shouting at the reader.
2. Don't return a letter to its sender by writing on it to save time or paper. A reply should be on a separate piece of paper, even if it's a short note. Contracts and other agreements are a separate issue.
3. Don't write "Thank you in advance." If you want to thank people in a request, simply make the request and then write "Thank you." Also, be sure to say thanks (perhaps in person) again when the task has been completed.
4. Don't use BCC on an e-mail unless you are quite sure that it is necessary. It could get you a bad reputation as being indiscreet.
5. Don't use tiny or unusual fonts that make your writing hard to read or that make you seem flippant.
6. Don't write a very long topic in the subject line of an e-mail.
7. Don't write a thank-you note on a card with a preprinted "Thank you!" or "Merci" (it's not considered good manners).
8. Don't let the passage of time stop you from writing to express congratulations, gratitude,

condolences, or whatever other sentiment your instincts say you *ought* to express.

9. Don't write a letter in anger or frustration. Step back, take some time, and detach yourself from the situation. Come back to writing when you have had time to reflect on the matter and can express yourself calmly.

10. Don't put anything in writing that you would be ashamed to see reported on the front page of the *Wall Street Journal.*

Appendix F

A Primer of Good Usage

abstruse. See **obtuse.**

accede; exceed. *Accede* = to agree or yield <We acceded to your request>. *Exceed* = to surpass, to be greater than <Your needs exceeded our capacity for production>.

access; excess. Both are traditionally nouns. *Access* = the act or opportunity of approaching or entering. *Excess* = an amount beyond what is required. Of course, *access* is also common today as a verb meaning "to gain entry to; to penetrate" <I couldn't access those files> <I accessed the storage unit>.

accord; accordance. *Accord* = agreement <The partners are in accord about expanding plant capacity>. *Accordance* = conformance <The materials weren't in accordance with our specs>.

administer; administrate. The first is standard. Avoid **administrate*, a back-formation from *administration.*

admission; admittance. *Admission* = permission or authority to enter <The price of admission is steep>. *Admittance* = physical entry <No admittance after 6 p.m.>.

adopt; adapt. *Adopt* = take up as one's own <Adopt this cause>. *Adapt* = modify <Adapt your leadership style>. Note that the nouns are *adoption* and *adaptation.*

adverse; averse. *Adverse* = unfavorable or contrary to <The expansion plan was postponed in face of adverse market conditions>. *Averse* = reluctant or unwilling; having distaste of, fear of, or hostility toward <The company is risk-averse>.

advise; advice. *Advise* is the verb <Our CFO advised against the merger>. *Advice* is the noun <We took the consultant's advice>.

affect; effect. *Affect* is usually a verb meaning "to have an influence" <The ordinance may affect our sales>. *Effect* is usually a noun denoting a result or outcome <It may be a positive effect>. *Effect* may also be a verb meaning "to bring about" <The new manager effected several changes>.

aggravate; irritate. *Aggravate* = to make worse <This news aggravates an already-bad situation>. *Irritate* = to annoy. Using *aggravate* to mean "irritate" is a common colloquialism, but it will still annoy some readers.

aide; aid. *Aide* is an assistant. *Aid* is assistance.

allusion; illusion. *Allusion* = an indirect reference, as to a cultural work, historical event, or other form of shared knowledge <"Sage of Omaha" is an allusion to Warren Buffett>. *Illusion* = a misperception or a mistaken belief <Their profitability turned out to be an illusion>.

a lot. Always two words.

already; all ready. *Already* = previously, by this time <She was already taking notes>. *All ready* = completely prepared <The corporate minutes were all ready for the secretary's sign-off>.

alternative; alternate. As a noun, *alternative* = one option (among one or more others) <We came up with an alternative design>; *alternate* = a substitute <The delegate's alternate attended>.

altogether; all together. *Altogether* = entirely or completely <This trip was altogether useless>. *All together* = collectively or in a group <That day we reported to him all together>.

ambiguous; ambivalent. *Ambiguous* = inviting more than one reasonable interpretation <Please clarify the

ambiguous policy>. *Ambivalent* = having mixed emotions about something <The CFO has ambivalent feelings about the trade-off>.

amend; emend. *Amend* = to add to a document, esp. a law or other legal document <Amend the contract>. *Emend* = to make corrections or edits to a piece of writing <Emend the proposal before you circulate it>.

among. See **between.**

amuse; bemuse. *Amuse* = to entertain or delight. *Bemuse* = to befuddle.

antidote; anecdote. *Antidote* = anything that counteracts a bad situation <Preparation is the antidote for nervousness>. *Anecdote* = an amusing, illustrative story <She told an anecdote about her first day on the job>.

anxious; eager. *Anxious* = anticipating with unease or worry <We grew anxious about the IPO>. *Eager* = anticipating with enthusiasm <Customers were eager for the retail stores to open>.

appraise; apprise. *Appraise* = to assess in value <Appraise the property at $1 million>. *Apprise* = to keep someone informed <Apprise me of any changes>.

arbiter; arbitrator. *Arbiter* = a person with final say over a matter <You're the arbiter of company policy>. *Arbitrator* = a person who conducts an arbitration to settle a dispute <The arbitrator decided the dispute in our favor>.

as. See **like.**

assure; ensure; insure. *Assure* = to try to satisfy someone of something <He assured me he'd attend>. *Ensure* = to make certain that something will happen or that things will be as expected <We made a schedule to ensure that we'd meet our deadline>. *Insure* = to indemnify against loss or damage <The warehouse was insured for less than market value>.

attain; obtain. *Attain* = to achieve or accomplish something <The regional division attained its quarterly sales target>. *Obtain* = to get something <We had no trouble obtaining raw materials>.

averse. See **adverse.**

avocation. See **vocation.**

awhile; a while. *Awhile* is an adverb meaning "for a short time" <Let's talk awhile before deciding>. *A while* is a noun phrase meaning "a period of time" <Let's talk for a while before deciding>.

bear; born; borne. *Bear* = (1) to carry or support <Corporate suitors come bearing gifts> or (2) to give birth <bear a child>. *Borne* refers to sense 1 <Airborne particulates make the product unsafe>, and *born* to sense 2 <You're a born leader>.

bemuse. See **amuse.**

beside; besides. *Beside* = (1) next to or at the side of <The seat beside the window is taken> or (2) outside of <That's beside the point> <she was beside herself with joy>. *Besides* = in addition to <Besides coffee, we sell tea and baked goods>.

between; among. *Between* shows one-to-one connections <Between payroll and health care, our costs are up>, even when more than two things are involved <Talks began between the firm and its various suitors>. *Among* connotes a looser relationship with three or more <There was one standout among applicants>.

blatant; flagrant. *Blatant* = obvious, overt <That's a blatant lie>. *Flagrant* = conspicuously rude or abusive <Refusing to shake hands was a flagrant break of protocol>.

bombastic = pompous, pretentious <Bombastic speeches stretched out the meeting>. The word has nothing to do with violence.

born; borne. See **bear.**

breach; broach. *Breach* = to break <That's a breach of contract> or break though <Expansion plans will breach the market's boundaries>. *Broach* = to bring up <I hate to broach the subject>.

can; may. Most properly, *can* expresses power or ability <We can ship your order next week>. *May* expresses permission or possibility <May we ship your order by UPS?>.

canvas; canvass. *Canvas* = coarse cloth <We ordered a canvas awning>. *Canvass* = a noun meaning "a poll or survey" or a verb meaning "to conduct a poll or survey" <Canvass your customers before you brainstorm new products>.

capital; Capitol. *Capitol* = the building where the U.S. Congress or a state legislature meets. In all other senses, the spelling is *capital* <capital expenses> <capital letter> <a capital crime> <the capital city>.

censor; censure. *Censor* = to inspect and possibly restrict the release of matter judged to be objectionable. *Censure* = to reprimand someone.

clench; clinch. *Clench* = to tighten, esp. in anger or determination <clenched fist>. *Clinch* = to secure or fasten <clinch the sale>.

climatic; climactic. *Climatic* = of the weather, esp. climate <climatic change>. *Climactic* = dramatic, riveting, moving toward a climax <climactic tension>.

clinch. See **clench.**

closure; cloture. *Closure* = the act or fact of concluding or resolving. *Cloture* = the parliamentary procedure for ending debate and calling for a vote.

collaborate; corroborate. *Collaborate* = to cooperate in an enterprise <We once collaborated in a joint venture>. *Corroborate* = to lend support, esp. by confirming information <Two studies corroborate the claims>.

common. See **mutual.**

compare to; compare with. To compare something *to* something else is to liken the two things; to compare it *with* something else is to note both similarities and differences.

compel; impel. *Compel* = to force, esp. by dint of authority or necessity <I felt compelled to report the error>. *Impel* = to drive forward, as by circumstances or weight of argument <Better opportunities impelled her to relocate>.

compendious; voluminous. *Compendious* = concise, condensed. *Voluminous* = large, roomy.

complementary; complimentary. *Complementary* = (1) making complete or perfect or (2) matching or harmonious <a bundle of complementary products>. *Complimentary* = (1) free <complimentary tickets> or (2) flattering <complimentary reviews>.

comprise; compose. *Comprise* = to include <The company comprises three business units>. *Compose* = to make up <The company is composed of three business units>. The phrase **is comprised of* is always faulty.

compulsive; compulsory. *Compulsive* = prone to or caused by uncontrollable urges <compulsive behavior>. *Compulsory* = mandatory <compulsory training>.

connote. See **denote.**

consequent; subsequent. *Consequent* = following as a result (consequence) <Our supplier took responsibility for consequent costs>. *Subsequent* = following in time <Subsequent ads included a disclaimer>.

continual; continuous. *Continual* = recurring, intermittent <continual calls for tech support>. *Continuous* = ceaseless, uninterrupted <continuous efforts to meet our goals>.

convince; persuade. *Convince . . . of* = to win over, to prove a point <convince the board of the need to expand>. *Persuade . . . to* = convince and cause to take action <persuade the board to fund the building program>.

corroborate. See **collaborate.**

council; counsel. *Council* = a board <the city council>. *Counsel* = (1) adviser <corporate counsel>, (2) advice <She heeded the counsel of her CFO>, or (3) to advise <My mentor counseled patience>.

credible; credulous; incredulous; creditable. *Credible* = believable, trustworthy <a credible argument>. *Credulous* = gullible <credulous acceptance>. *Incredulous* =

unbelieving <an incredulous audience>. *Creditable* = respectable but not outstanding <a creditable performance>.

damage; damages. *Damage* = harm <damage caused by the false rumor>. *Damages* = judicial compensation for harm <judgment for $2 million in damages>.

declaim. See **disclaim.**

definite; definitive. *Definite* = clear, explicit, unmistakable <a definite asset to the department>. *Definitive* = authoritative <the definitive source of information>.

delegate. See **relegate.**

deliberate; deliberative. *Deliberate* = purposeful <a deliberate affront>. *Deliberative* = of or relating to debate or discussion <a deliberative decision-making process>.

denote; connote. *Denote* = to signify; to be the name of <*Mortgagee* denotes the lender, not the borrower>. *Connote* = to imply; to suggest something beyond the literal sense of a term <An open workspace connotes collaboration>.

depreciate; deprecate. *Depreciate* = to fall in value <The car will depreciate by 40% when you drive it away>. *Deprecate* = to disapprove of, to plead against <The manager deprecated the use of company meal allowances for those working solo>.

detract; distract. *Detract* = take away (some quality) <His abrupt manner detracted from his effectiveness>. *Distract* = divert <An accomplice distracted the cashier>.

device; devise. *Device* = a tool or apparatus <a handy device>. *Devise* = to create or invent <devise a better system>.

different. Prefer *different from* over *different than.*

differ from; differ with. To *differ from* is simply to be different <Gross profits differ from net profits>; to *differ with* is to disagree <I differ with you on that point>.

disburse. See **disperse.**

disclaim; declaim. *Disclaim* = deny or disavow <disclaim any knowledge of the report>. *Declaim* = to orate <declaim against corruption>.

discrete; discreet. *Discrete* = distinct <three discrete sources of funding>. *Discreet* = circumspect, tactful <a discreet phone call>.

disinterested; uninterested. *Disinterested* = unbiased; lacking any financial or emotional stake in a dispute <The arbitrator must be a disinterested third party>. *Uninterested* = uncaring <The audience was uninterested>.

disperse; disburse. *Disperse* = to scatter <disperse an unruly crowd>. *Disburse* = to distribute funds <disburse grants>.

distinct; distinctive. *Distinct* = clear, well-defined <We set three distinct goals this quarter>. *Distinctive* = marking a difference, characteristic <her distinctive management style is unlike any we've ever seen>.

distract. See **detract.**

dominant; dominate. *Dominant* = supreme <the dominant player>. *Dominate* = to control <dominate the market>.

eager. See **anxious.**

effect. See **affect.**

e.g.; i.e. *E.g.* = for example <big-ticket items (e.g., cars, refrigerators, and furnaces)>. *I.e.* = that is <numismatics (i.e., coin-collecting)>.

elicit; illicit. *Elicit* = to draw a response <The verbal gaffe elicited laughter>. *Illicit* = forbidden, illegal <illicit behavior>.

eligible; illegible. *Eligible* = fit to be chosen; suitable. *Illegible* = incapable of being read because of bad handwriting, poor printing, etc.

embarrass. So spelled.

emend. See **amend.**

eminent. See **imminent.**

empathy; sympathy. *Empathy* = understanding <empathy for a kindred spirit>. *Sympathy* = compassion <sympathy for the displaced survivors>.

ensure. See **assure.**

equally. Avoid *equally as*. Good usage dictates *equally profitable,* not **equally as profitable.*

evoke; invoke. *Evoke* = to draw out <evoke memories>. *Invoke* = to call on, esp. for authority or assistance <invoke the right to counsel>.

explicit; implicit. *Explicit* = (1) unambiguous <an explicit disclaimer> or (2) graphic, lurid <explicit photos>. *Implicit* = (1) implied <an implicit warranty> or (2) absolute <implicit trust>.

farther; further. *Farther* = physically more distant <Drive three miles farther>. *Further* = more advanced <Further study is needed>.

faze; phase. *Faze* = to agitate <not fazed by the rude caller>. *Phase* = a stage of development <a growing phase>.

fewer. See **less.**

first, second, third. So written—preferably not **firstly,* **secondly,* **thirdly.*

flagrant. See **blatant.**

flair; flare. *Flair* = (1) an innate talent <a flair for pitching ideas> or (2) stylishness <write with flair>. *Flare* = a burst, as of light, activity, etc. <an emotional flare-up>.

flaunt; flout. *Flaunt* = to show off something <flaunting new jewelry>. Flout = to openly disobey or disregard <flouting the rules>.

flounder; founder. *Flounder* = to struggle or thrash about <The campaign was floundering>. *Founder* = (1) to sink <The stock foundered when profits fell> or (2) to fail <The company foundered after the scandal>.

forbear; forebear. *Forbear* = to refrain from an impulse <We must forbear any thoughts of retaliating>. *Forebear* = an ancestor <My grandmother and other forebears were mostly Irish>.

forgo; forego. *Forgo* = to do without <forgo help>. *Forego* = to precede <the foregoing events>.

formally; formerly. *Formally* = properly <We haven't been formally introduced>. *Formerly* = previously <He was formerly with Hastings>.

founder. See **flounder.**

further. See **farther.**

gibe; jibe. *Gibe* = a taunt or tease <The manager's talk was interrupted by good-natured gibes>. *Jibe* = agree <That jibes with what I expected>.

harass. So spelled.

horde; hoard. *Horde* = large group of people <hordes of customers>. *Hoard* = a cache, esp. of valuable things <a hoard of cash>. As a verb, to *hoard* is to accumulate to an excessive degree.

i.e. See **e.g.**

if; whether. A fine but useful distinction: *If* = on the condition that. So, e.g., *Let me know if you need a catalog* means most rigorously not to call if you don't want a catalog. *Whether* = which way you decide about. So *Let me know whether you need a catalog* means, again most rigorously, to please call either way.

illegible. See **eligible.**

illicit. See **elicit.**

illusion. See **allusion.**

imminent; eminent. *Imminent* = looming and inevitable <an imminent announcement>. *Eminent* = prominent and respected <an eminent authority on the subject>.

impel. See **compel.**

implicit. See **explicit.**

imply; infer. *Imply* = to suggest something without saying it expressly <There's an implied threat>. *Infer* = to read into <Can we infer from the announcement that they will build stores close to ours?>.

in behalf of. See **on behalf of.**

incredulous. See **credible.**

infer. See **imply.**

ingenious; ingenuous. *Ingenious* = clever, skillful <That is an ingenious solution>. *Ingenuous* = frank, innocent, free of ulterior motive <Security released the child, who they said was open and ingenuous under questioning>.

in order to. Usually you can shorten this expression to *to.* Do so whenever you can with no loss in clarity.

insure. See **assure.**

invoke. See **evoke.**

irritate. See **aggravate.**

it's; its. *It's* = it is <it's no mistake>. *Its* = the possessive form of *it* <each branch has its responsibilities>.

jibe. See **gibe.**

just deserts (what one deserves) is so spelled—not **just desserts. Deserve* and *desert* [pronounced /di-ZURT/] are related words.

lay > laid > laid. To *lay* is to put down or arrange <I'll lay it on his desk> <I laid it on his desk yesterday> <if only I'd laid it there>.

lend; loan. *Lend* = to provide, to grant the temporary use of <Could you lend me that calculator?>. *Loan* = a sum of money that has been lent <We're paying back the loan>. Though traditionally a noun, *loan* is also acceptable as a verb when the object is money <We asked the bank to loan us $50,000>.

less; fewer. *Less* = a smaller amount <less waste>. *Fewer* = a smaller number <fewer losses>.

lie > lay > lain. To *lie* is to recline <I should lie down> <I lay down earlier this afternoon> <if I'd lain down this afternoon, I'd have more energy now>.

like; as. *Like* precedes a noun or pronoun <like a rock>. *As* precedes a subject and verb <as you said>.

loan. See **lend.**

loathe; loath. *Loathe* is the verb meaning "to abhor" <He loathes broccoli>. *Loath* is the adjective meaning "reluctant" <He's loath to admit that he loves spinach>.

loose; lose. *Loose* is an adjective meaning “not tight” or “not constrained” <loose lips> or a verb meaning “to free” <loose the dogs of war>. *Lose,* the verb <lose customers>, is often misspelled *loose.*

make do = to get by with <We’ll have to make do with what’s available>. The phrase is often mistakenly rendered **make due.*

marshal. Both the noun <the fire marshal> and the verb <marshal our arguments> are so spelled.

may. See **can.**

mete out = to allocate. So rendered, not **meet out.*

militate. See **mitigate.**

minuscule = tiny <a minuscule amount>. So spelled, not **miniscule.*

mitigate; militate. *Mitigate* = to make less harsh <I normally would have filed a complaint, but there were mitigating circumstances>. *Militate* = to weight heavily in one direction <A long history of conflict militated against the agreement>.

mutual; common. *Mutual* = reciprocal <mutual admiration>. *Common* = shared <common interests>.

nonplussed = frozen by surprise, perplexed <nonplussed by the shocking news>.

number. See **quantity.**

obtain. See **attain.**

obtuse; abstruse. *Obtuse* = dull, dim-witted <I was too obtuse to catch the allusion>. *Abstruse* = obscure, arcane <But it turns out that no one caught the abstruse allusion>.

on behalf of; in behalf of. *On behalf of* = representing <accepting the award on behalf of>. *In behalf of* = in support of <speaking in behalf of the motion>.

orient; *orientate. *Orient* = to get one's bearings <spend the first day getting oriented>. **Orientate* is an ostentatious variant to be avoided.

past; passed. *Past* is the noun <in the past>, adjective <past efforts>, adverb <walk on past>, and preposition <past the park>. *Passed* is the past tense and past participle of the verb *pass* <time passed slowly>.

peak; peek; pique. *Peak* = a high point, esp. a pointed one such as a mountaintop or a spike on a chart <reach the peak>. *Peek* = a quick, furtive look <take a peek at this file>. *Pique* = (1) indignation <a fit of pique> or (2) to arouse <piqued her interest>.

peddle; pedal. *Peddle* = to sell <peddle hot dogs>. *Pedal* = to operate a foot lever <pedal a bike>.

peek. See **peak.**

pejorative = having negative implications; tending to belittle. So spelled, not _*perjorative._

pendant; pendent. *Pendant* = a piece of dangling jewelry <a silver pendant>. *Pendent* = pending, unsettled <a pendent lawsuit>.

people. See **persons.**

percent. This word (meaning "by the hundred") was formerly spelled as two words. Today it is one.

perquisite; prerequisite. *Perquisite* = a privilege or benefit, esp. one attached to a position; usually shortened to *perk* <Perks included a company car>. *Prerequisite* = a necessary condition <This position has job-training prerequisites>.

persecute; prosecute. *Persecute* = treat harshly, esp. as a group <a persecuted minority>. *Prosecute* = pursue legal action <prosecuted for embezzlement >.

personal; personnel. *Personal* = an adjective meaning "private, individual." *Personnel* = a noun meaning "the whole group of persons employed in a business."

persuade. See **convince.**

persons; people. In most contexts, the plural *persons* sounds stilted. Except for set phrases <missing-persons report>, reserve *person* for singular use <Only one person showed up> and use *people* for the plural.

perspicuous; perspicacious. *Perspicuous* = lucid <a perspicuous argument>. *Perspicacious* = insightful, shrewd <a perspicacious observer of the market>.

phase. See **faze.**

pique. See **peak.**

populace; populous. *Populace* = the inhabitants of a place, collectively <the Swiss populace>. *Populous* = heavily populated <populous northeastern cities>.

pore; pour. To *pore* is to read intently <poring over the financial statements>. To *pour* is to make (a liquid) flow downward.

practical; practicable. *Practical* = pertaining to experience or actual use; adapted to useful action instead of to contemplation <There must be a practical way of shipping these goods>. *Practicable* = capable of being done or used <Scientists have long known that a perpetual-motion machine is impracticable>.

precede; proceed. *Precede* = to occur before something else <An extensive campaign preceded the launch>. **Preceed* is a common misspelling. *Proceed* = (1) to start <Proceed with your report> or (2) to continue <From St. Louis, proceed to Chicago>.

precipitate; precipitous. *Precipitate* is most commonly a verb meaning "to cause suddenly or recklessly" <precipitate a riot>. As an adjective, it means "sudden, rash, or violent" <a precipitate run on the banks>. *Precipitous* = steep <a precipitous decline in demand>.

prerequisite. See **perquisite.**

prescribe; proscribe. *Prescribe* = to direct a course of action <The consultants prescribed a plan>. *Proscribe* = to forbid or outlaw <Insider trading is proscribed>.

presumptive; presumptuous. *Presumptive* = assumed to be <the presumptive nominee>. *Presumptuous* = arrogant, impudent <making presumptuous demands>.

preventive; *preventative. *Preventive* = intended to ward off harm <preventive measures>. **Preventative* is a corrupt form.

principal; principle. *Principal* = main, first <the principal reason>. As a noun, it refers to the main person <a principal at a consulting firm> or, in finance, the original sum of money lent or invested <the principal continues to earn interest>. *Principle* = a belief, tenet, or law <stand on principle> <the principles of economics>.

proceed. See **precede.**

prophesy; prophecy. *Prophesy* = to predict <prophesy great success>. *Prophecy* = the prediction <another doomsday prophecy>.

proposition; proposal. *Proposition* = something that is offered for consideration <We reject the proposition that

plants should be located only on rivers>. *Proposal* = a formal offer <His proposal was silent on the personnel required to make it work>.

proscribe. See **prescribe.**

prosecute. See **persecute.**

prostrate; prostate. *Prostrate* = lying face down. *Prostate* = a gland in male mammals.

proved; proven. *Proved* = the long-preferred past participle of *prove* <last year's financial projections have proved accurate>. An exception is the set phrase *innocent until proven guilty. Proven* is an adjective <Our new software line is already a proven seller in the market>.

quandary = state of confusion <in a quandary about how to proceed>, not the cause of that confusion.

quantity; number. *Quantity* = an unspecified mass <The farm produces large quantities of grain>. *Number* = a collection of individually countable objects <The number of units we sold last year exceeded that of any previous year>.

rack. See **wrack.**

rebut; refute. *Rebut* = to answer a charge or argument. *Refute* = to disprove a charge or argument.

reek; wreak. *Reek* = (1) to stink <The stagnant water reeks> or (2) the bad odor <We could smell the reek of an open sewer>. *Wreak* = to cause a specified type of harm <wreak havoc>.

refute. See **rebut.**

regrettable; regretful. *Regrettable* = unfortunate <a regrettable decision>. *Regretful* = sorry about <regretful about not calling>.

rein; reign. *Rein* = a bridle strap. Figuratively, the means of control <give free rein> <to rein in>. The homophone *reign* (= to rule over) is sometimes mistakenly used in those and similar idioms.

relegate; delegate. *Relegate* = to reassign to a lower position or task <relegated to traffic control>. *Delegate* = to entrust (a person) to act on one's behalf <delegated the research to Terry>.

reluctant. See **reticent.**

respectfully; respectively. *Respectfully* = in a polite manner <May I respectfully ask you to wait another five minutes>. *Respectively* = in regular order <So $500,000 and $600,000 are the benchmarks, respectively, for Ted and Carol>.

reticent; reluctant. *Reticent* = taciturn, not open about one's thought; reluctant to talk <Veterans can be reticent

about their experiences>. Avoid using it as a substitute for being *reluctant* to act.

role; roll. *Role* (in the sense "a part in an organization, a movie, etc.") and *roll* (in the sense "a list of participants, actors, etc.") are often confounded.

sanction = (1) a penalty <The commission imposed sanctions for the incident> or (2) an endorsement <The board gave its sanction for continued talks>.

species; specie. *Species* = a type of plant or animal. The word is both singular and plural. *Specie* = coined money.

stanch. See **staunch.**

stationary; stationery. *Stationary* = unmoving <The gym has five stationary bikes>. *Stationery* = writing paper <We received 12 boxes of stationery>.

staunch; stanch. *Staunch* = loyal and devoted <He's a staunch supporter>. *Stanch* = to stop or control the actual or figurative loss of liquid <stanch the red ink>.

strait; straight. *Strait* = a tight spot <Strait of Magellan> <in dire straits>. *Straight* often displaces *strait* in *straitjacket* and *straitlaced.*

strategy; tactics. *Strategy* = big-picture planning <competitive strategy>. *Tactics* = actions and techniques that support your strategy <flash mobs and other guerrilla-marketing tactics>.

subsequent. See **consequent.**

supersede = to take the place of <It supersedes last year's employee handbook>. The word is often misspelled **supercede.*

sympathy. See **empathy.**

tactics. See **strategy.**

than. See **then.**

that; which. Use *that* to introduce a clause that's essential to meaning (a restrictive clause), and don't set it off with commas. If you write, "The departments that made their numbers last quarter received budget increases," readers will infer that some departments didn't receive increases. Use *which* with a clause that isn't essential (a nonrestrictive clause). If you write, "The departments, which made their numbers last quarter, received budget increases," you're saying that all departments received increases. You can leave out a *which* clause set off by commas and still convey the gist of the sentence.

their. See **there.**

then; than. *Then* = at that time; in that case; therefore. *Than* expresses comparison <more successful than any other start-up>.

there; their; they're. *There* refers to direction <over there> or place <where there is life>; *their* is the possessive of *they* <all their worldly belongings>; and *they're* is the contraction of *they are* <they're on the way>.

torpid. See **turgid.**

toward; towards. *Toward* dominates in American English, *towards* in British English.

try and. Make it **try to.**

turgid; torpid. *Turgid* = (1) swollen <the turgid river after Friday's rain>, or (2) bombastic <a turgid harangue>. *Torpid* = dormant or sluggish <Demand is usually torpid after the holidays>.

uninterested. See **disinterested.**

unique; unusual. *Unique* = one of a kind, unmatched <a unique handmade quilt>. As an absolute term, *unique* should not take modifiers such as *very.* It is not a synonym of *unusual.*

use; utilize. Prefer the simple term.

venal; venial. *Venal* = corrupt, susceptible to bribery <a venal border guard>. *Venial* = pardonable <a venial mistake>.

veracity; voracity. *Veracity* = truthfulness <Veracity earns trust>. *Voracity* = gluttony <His voracity was his downfall>.

verbiage = wordiness, not the words in a message. *Excess verbiage* is redundant. Avoid the misspelling **verbage.*

vocation; avocation. *Vocation* = career <His vocation is nursing>. *Avocation* = (1) hobby or (2) second occupation <On weekends he works on his avocation, flint-knapping>.

voluminous. See **compendious.**

voracity. See **veracity.**

wangle. See **wrangle.**

whether. See **if.**

whether; whether or not. In most instances *whether* can stand alone: *or not* adds nothing. But when the sense is "regardless of whether," the additional words are needed <We're going whether or not you can make it>.

which. See **that.**

who's; whose. *Who's* = who is. *Whose* = the possessive form of *who* or *whom.*

whosever; whoever's. *Whosever* is the standard possessive form of *whoever. Whoever's* is a contraction for *whoever is.*

workers' compensation. This gender-neutral phrase has replaced *workmen's compensation* as standard.

wrack; rack. *Wrack* = (1) to destroy <wracked by fraud> or (2) wreckage <go to wrack and ruin>. *Rack* = to torture as on a rack <rack my brains>.

wrangle; wangle. *Wrangle* = to argue noisily <wrangling over licensing rights>. *Wangle* = to obtain by manipulation <wangle an invitation>.

wreak. See **reek.**

your; you're. *Your* = possessive form of *you. You're* = contraction of *you are.*

Desk References

Writing well is not just one skill but a combination of many—and it's something you must constantly work at. In addition to this guide you might want to keep the following desk references handy.

The Basic Writer's Bookshelf

- *The American Heritage Dictionary of the English Language.* 5th ed. Boston: Houghton Mifflin Harcourt, 2011.
- Garner, Bryan A. *Garner's Dictionary of Modern American Usage.* 3d ed. New York: Oxford, 2009.
- *Merriam-Webster's Collegiate Dictionary.* 11th ed. Springfield, MA: Merriam-Webster, 2008.
- *Roget's Thesaurus of English Words and Phrases.* George Davidson, ed. Avon, MA: Adams Media, 2011.
- Trimble, John R. *Writing with Style.* 3d ed. Upper Saddle River, NJ: Pearson, 2010.

The Connoisseur's Bookshelf

- Flesch, Rudolf. *The Art of Plain Talk*. New York: Harper & Brothers, 1946.
- Flesch, Rudolf. *How to Write Plain English: A Book for Lawyers and Consumers*. New York: Harper & Row, 1979.
- Fowler, H. W. *A Dictionary of Modern English Usage*. 2d ed. Edited by Ernest Gowers. New York: Oxford University Press, 1965.
- Garner, Bryan A. *Legal Writing in Plain English*. 2d ed. Chicago: University of Chicago Press, 2013.
- Gowers, Ernest. *The Complete Plain Words*. 3d ed. Edited by Sidney Greenbaum and Janet Whitcut. Boston: David R. Godine, 1986.
- Graves, Robert, and Alan Hodge. *The Reader over Your Shoulder*. 2d ed. London: Cape, 1947.
- Partridge, Eric. *Usage and Abusage: A Guide to Good English*. New York: Harper & Brothers, 1942.
- Strunk, William, and E. B. White. *The Elements of Style*. 4th ed. Boston: Allyn & Bacon, 1999.
- Tufte, Edward R. *Beautiful Evidence*. Cheshire, Conn.: Graphics Press, 2006.
- Tufte, Edward R. *Envisioning Information*. Cheshire, Conn.: Graphics Press, 1990.

- Wallace, David Foster. *Consider the Lobster.* New York: Little, Brown & Co., 2005.
- Zinsser, William. *On Writing Well.* New York: HarperCollins, 30th Ann. ed., 2006.

Index

Acknowledgments

My profound gratitude goes to Lisa Burrell of HBR, who suggested and edited the book through several revisions; to the LawProse employees Heather C. Haines, Becky R. McDaniel, Tiger Jackson, Jeff Newman, David Zheng, and Ryden McComas Anderson—all of whom helped in developing and refining the text; my Twitter followers (I'm @bryanagarner) who suggested examples of bizspeak to be avoided; my mother-in-law Sandra W. Cheng, her brother Daniel Wu, and my sister-in-law Linda Garner, all of whom suggested lines of inquiry from their many years in business; and most of all my wife, Karolyne H.C. Garner, who cheered and goaded and inspired me in the months when this book was being written—as she has before and since.

The book is dedicated to J.P. Allen, the filmmaker, who has been my close friend from childhood (I was 5, he was 3): We developed our interest in language and writing as teenagers, while also reading intensively about entrepreneurship and business management—never worrying that we might be considered nerds or eggheads. We always thought learning was cool, and ignorance uncool. Nothing has changed.

B.A.G.

August 2012

About the Author

Bryan A. Garner is a noted lexicographer, grammarian, lawyer, and business owner. Since founding LawProse Inc. in 1991, he has trained more than 150,000 lawyers in the techniques of written persuasion and effective contract drafting. His clients include the legal departments of dozens of *Fortune* 500 companies.

Garner is the author of *Garner's Modern American Usage, The Elements of Legal Style,* and *The Winning Brief,* and the editor in chief of all in-print editions of *Black's Law Dictionary.* He has coauthored two best-selling books about judicial decision-making with Justice Antonin Scalia.

Notes

Notes

Notes

Notes

Notes

Notes

Notes